TALK WITH YOUR KIDS

FOR FIONA

ACKNOWLEDGMENTS

Jeremy Madin and Helen Nugent at Cranbrook for their backing of this program from the outset. Jane Curry Publishing and the people at Black Dog and Leventhal for picking up the idea and running with it. Phillip Cam, Sandy Lynch, and all those in the Philosophy in Schools Association over the years. Rod Farraway, Christophe Gauchat, Peter Hipwell, Anne Robertson, and all those who have helped in their discussions relating to these conversations. Thanks also to Jonah Darling for many of the photographs and to Jill Corcoran, my agent. My parents and my teachers for giving me whatever ethical sense that I may have. My wife Fiona for many conversations about Conversations. And to my children Julia and Elena.

A percentage of author royalties from the sale of this book goes to fund Cranbrook/Jeremy Madin School in the foothills of Nepal.

Note: A version of many of these materials form the base of the Ethics program at Cranbrook School in Sydney, Australia. I thank the hundred teachers and the thousand students who have had these discussions and given me such useful feedback. In particular I thank the several hundred boys who have challenged me in 109 and more ethics conversations over the past four years.

Originally published by Jane Curry Publishing under the title
Ethics: 101 Conversations to Have with Your Kids

ISBN: 978-1-57912-948-4

Library of Congress Cataloging-in-Publication Data
on file at the offices of Black Dog & Leventhal Publishers, Inc.

Manufactured in the United States

Published by Black Dog & Leventhal Publishers, Inc.
151 West 19th Street New York, New York 10011

Distributed by Workman Publishing Company 225 Varick Street New York, New York 10014

Photography: Jonah Darling; stock.xchng; and Shutterstock.com

b c d e f g h i

talk with your kids

109 CONVERSATIONS ABOUT ETHICS AND
THINGS THAT REALLY MATTER

MICHAEL PARKER

BLACK DOG
& LEVENTHAL
PUBLISHERS

CONTENTS

INTRODUCTION

WHY THIS BOOK?

Your child may be smart but is he or she good?

Many families and almost all schools spend a great deal of time academically developing their children. This is a good thing. Yet I think it is at least as important for us to all think consciously about how we ethically develop the next generation to be decent members of society. This development already bubbles under the surface in homes and schools, but we can make this development break through the surface and become explicit. This can be done with lots of complex problems, lots of the wisdom of the ages, and lots of independent thinking—all of which this book serves up.

WHERE DO CHILDREN GET THEIR VALUES?

Of course, I must start with the observation that if you don't own this book, your children are not necessarily destined to become unethical brutes. Children learn their ethics from all parts of the world around them: sometimes from school, their friends, their church, their sports team, or their ballet class. Children don't learn ethics by getting it in a handbook.

The main place that a child learns his or her system of ethics is from the home (no pressure, Mom and Dad.) This should come as no great surprise to anyone—home is where a child spends most of his or her formative years.

Children will learn consideration from how considerate their parents are. They will learn empathy from how much their parents care. They will learn generosity from watching how generous their parents are to others. It has always been so. In addition, basic ethics are still delivered by parents in everyday interactions. "Share that toy with your sister," "Wait your turn" are all ethical instructions, taught in an unremarkable way in most homes a dozen times a day.

Ethically strong parents still can have children who cheat, lie, and push old ladies over in the street—after all parents are not a child's only source of instruction. However, the positive example of parenting is invaluable.

While this basic, practical, moral education has remained the same, what has changed in the last generation or two is the way in which ethics has been transmitted explicitly. Several major shifts have occurred.

Firstly, outside organizations such as churches often no longer play such a strong role in a child's life. Many religions in particular preach about how to live and the ethical statements they make are fundamental, involving charity, generosity, care, and purposefulness, for example "do unto others as you would have done unto yourself." However, the ethical teachings of religion as a moral compass are something that many children don't get anymore. You don't have to subscribe to any of the major religion's theistic beliefs to appreciate the value of many of the moral statements they taught.

Secondly, some parents now feel they have lost their authority to "push" ethical concepts on their children. Expecting or imposing firm ethical standards can make you feel like an old fashioned authoritarian; not merely "copying" your own parents, but copying your great great grandparents. And this hardly gives you street cred with your child or their friends. For example, insisting that "responsibilities are as fundamental as rights in a functioning society (e.g. this house)" may sound like nineteenth century twaddle. However, insisting that "the responsibility to do some housework is the flip side of the right to live in a house that is not a cesspit" is important.

Also, saying that "all opinions are equally valid" is often a cheap way of getting parents and teachers off the hook when the ethical questions get tough. This started several decades ago when, in some quarters, whatever values the child developed were acceptable. For example a child might say "My values are to look after only number one and trample whoever else is down," and for authority figures to intervene in this would be indoctrination. However, I think it is clear that not all ethical positions are equally good and that some values are better than others. Again, to use an example, when a small new boy turns up at your daughter's school without food it is NOT ethically equivalent for your daughter to share her lunch or punch him in the face. One is kind and the other is mean. Very little your child may reason to the contrary will change this fact. How to deal with this in a nuanced way in conversations is something I raise later, under "conversations with the ethically challenged child."

SO WHAT VALUES ARE WORTHWHILE?

In discussing the questions in this book with your children, you are no doubt hoping that they come to hold a "good" set of values. Sometimes though it can be tough to put your finger on exactly what some of those values might be. I have listed some values that you would probably want your children to keep developing as they get older (they also appear in Conversation 75).

It's unrealistic to expect someone to have all of these values. And you don't want to go over the top with some of them either—too much "assertiveness" for example can be a bad thing. Nonetheless it is a handy list to keep in mind.

Acceptance
Appreciation
Assertiveness
Awe
Benevolence
Caring
Charity
Cheerfulness
Commitment
Compassion
Confidence
Consideration
Contentment
Co-operation
Courage
Courtesy
Creativity
Curiosity
Determination
Devotion
Dignity
Diligence
Empathy
Enthusiasm
Fairness
Faith
Fidelity
Flexibility
Forgiveness

Fortitude
Friendliness
Generosity
Gentleness
Grace
Gratitude
Helpfulness
Honesty
Honor
Hope
Humanity
Humility
Humor
Idealism
Independence
Initiative
Integrity
Joyfulness
Justice
Kindness
Love
Loyalty
Mercy
Mindfulness
Moderation
Modesty
Openness
Optimism
Patience

Peacefulness
Perceptiveness
Perseverance
Purposefulness
Reliability
Resilience
Respect
Responsibility
Righteousness
Self-sacrifice
Self-discipline
Serenity
Service
Simplicity
Sincerity
Steadfastness
Strength
Tact
Thankfulness
Thoughtfulness
Tolerance
Trust
Trustworthiness
Truthfulness
Understanding
Wisdom
Wonder

THE VALUE OF DISCUSSION

Ethics and values should be spoken about regularly in homes. Often they already are. Every time your child comes home with an example of something "unfair" that happened at school, this is an opportunity to speak about ethics. When an issue comes up on television or in films, this is an opportunity to speak about ethics.

I am not suggesting a return to the "good old days" when children were simply told how to behave and be respectful. Indeed, I am almost suggesting the reverse. I am suggesting that ethical issues are discussed and pulled apart by the whole family in conversation and that your children are a central part in these conversations. However, this is not permissive "values clarification" either. Instead, the important thing here is a belief that certain values are generally better—that courage is better than cowardice, that generosity is better than selfishness—and the rightness of these values is exposed by conversation and free thinking.

For example, you can tell a child "You have to be tolerant of other people" and he or she will hear "parent static" and probably filter you out. But if you use situations and examples to discuss tolerance and guide them to their own conclusions, your child will probably come to the view that tolerance is preferable to intolerance. The difference is that your child will have articulated the view themselves. The opinion will be his or hers and s/he will own it. So, in short, the better way to make a child tolerant is not to tell them to be, but to make him or her think it themselves. Of course, better than each of these is to get them to practice tolerance—but this book can't engineer that.

In having thoughtful, ethical discussions with your children (instead of ramming ideas down their throat or letting them get away with any view at all) you are becoming a small part of the great enlightened tradition that has been going on for hundreds of years. It is the same tradition that bought you democracy, freedom of speech, the emancipation of slaves, and Monty Python. For centuries being enlightened means valuing the received wisdom of the ages. It has been proud of producing in people the ability to think critically. And it has been proud of allowing people to form their own well-grounded views by combining these other two elements. It charts the middle way between authoritarianism and permissiveness. Being open-minded is a rare and precious triumph of the human species that I think we are obliged to hand on to our children. In using this book, with all of its ethical thinking skills, philosophies, and dilemmas, you are doing exactly that.

Authoritarian	Enlightened	Permissive

On the one hand the conversations in this book might be a little awkward at the start. Lets not pretend that they are the same type of conversation as "How was your day?" or "Didn't the Giants crush the Patriots?" Yet consistently discussing ethics with your children is one of the most important things you can do. And look at it this way—millions of parents are out there at the moment drilling their children in extra comprehension, grammar and math questions that come from joyless workbooks. I doubt that these are producing engaged, quality discussions between parents and children. As an educational project, this book and the conversations it promotes are a whole lot more interesting and worthwhile.

HOW TO USE THIS BOOK

This book works the way you want it to work. You may choose to have a program of sitting at the dinner table one particular night every week and working from conversation to conversation. More likely you will dip in and out of conversations as they take your interest. You might choose a set time, or pull the book out occasionally. You may simply hand it to your children and say, "Which ones take your interest?" You may put it in the glove compartment of your car and pull it out when the road gets too long. You may keep this book in the background (in a drawer or by the bedside) and bring up the various dilemmas from memory when the times suit. You may take the ideas from the book and simply make up your own ethical dilemmas each time your child comes home from school with an issue. It is up to you.

Having said that, I do think it is important that your children get exposure to each of the three categories of conversations in the book.

- **Category 1**—the ethical dilemmas and questions.

- **Category 2**—the thinking-skills questions (10 of the conversations are like this: the ones ending in "0" i.e. 10, 20, 30).

- **Category 3**—what famous ethicists and philosophers have thought in the past (11 of the conversations are like this: the ones ending in "5" i.e. 15, 25, 35).

The most important skill for parents to learn is how to fan the flames of the conversation so that the discussions catch fire instead of go out. There are many ways to do this and I have listed a few here.

ASK MORE QUESTIONS

Once your child has put forward a point of view, you can ask them why they believe this or you can ask them to give an example. You can ask them to give reasons for their opinion. You can ask how it links with other ideas they have had. You can ask them how it is different from something their brother or sister has just said. Just keep asking questions. By doing this, you are shepherding them along and getting them to think about their own thinking. (By the way, the single word "Why?" is more likely to fan the flames of a discussion than anything else.)

Asking more questions can be harder than it sounds. You might want to jump in with your own opinion, which could well be a conversation killer. Sometimes you will have to bite your tongue and use questions to explore the point of view with your children. The more they get to speak, the more they will feel that their point of view is being valued and the more they will be willing to speak.

Some specific questions:

- "What would the world look like if everyone did that?"

- "Can you think of an opposite example?"

- "How would you feel if you were on the other side of that?"

- "Have you got another reason for that?"

- "Who gets advantaged by that? Who gets disadvantaged? Is that fair?"

- "What do you think your football coach/priest/teacher/rabbi/ school principal would think about that?"

- "What harm does this decision create? Is it worth it?"

- "Even if no harm has been created, could it still be wrong?"

- "Why?"

- "Why?"

PLAY "DEVIL'S ADVOCATE"

This means coming up with the opposite opinion (e.g. if everyone in the family quickly decides that it is okay to tell a white lie to your granny who has knitted you a horrible sweater, then you can be the person to say that granny would rather know the truth so that she stopped wasting her time knitting more sweaters that no one likes). However, it is vitally important that your children know you are playing devil's advocate to keep the discussion going, instead of just disagreeing with them. Flat out disagreements may throw water on the fire of the conversation instead of keeping it going.

PRESENT OPPOSITE OPINIONS AS ALTERNATIVES

To keep the spirit of open inquiry alive you can use a lot of starters such as "Another way of looking at it is. . . ", "Another factor to think about is. . . ", "Another person might say. . . ", "Have you thought about it this way?", "Actually now that I think about it, you could also say. . . "

GET YOUR CHILD TO VOLUNTEER
EQUIVALENT EXAMPLES FROM REAL LIFE

Many of the conversations are about real world issues, such as bullying, lying, and cafeteria behavior, that your child may well have other examples of (e.g. the questions about bystander bullying may prompt them to talk about a time when they saw someone being bullied). These "real life" examples are probably more likely to fan a discussion, because they have experienced it. Once you have the real world examples, you can even leave the hypotheticals behind and get to the real world discussion. Other hypotheticals (e.g. would you torture a terrorism suspect) will not have real life analogues, unless your child is living a very interesting life.

CREATE A "SHADES OF GRAY" CATEGORY

As we know, a lot of situations are not clearly ethical or unethical. Instead, there are shades of gray. You can introduce this into discussions by using the terms "white," "light gray," "medium gray," "dark gray," etc. Something else you can do to get your children thinking about shades of gray is to have them "rank" situations from most to least acceptable. A lot of the conversations have about eight or ten different situations to discuss. These can be easily ranked.

GET YOUR CHILD TO PUT ON THE "MANTLE OF THE EXPERT"

This involves pretending that your children are experts. For example, you could say "Pretend you are the school principal and you have to make a decision" or "Pretend we are an Ethics Board that has been set up" or "Pretend you are the president." This simple trick gives a lot of questions more "oomph." I have used this trick for some of the discussions in this book, but you can use it for a lot more.

SHOW THEM YOU ARE INTERESTED IN THEIR OPINION

Children are more likely to have a discussion with you if they think you are taking what they say seriously. Showing you are interested involves actively listening. Do all the little conversation promoters such as "okay," "I see," and "right" as they are speaking. Nod as they speak. Ask them follow up questions. Don't look like you are waiting for their turn to be over so you can get back to delivering your point. Better still, BE interested in what they say, so that all of the conversation promoters come naturally.

SOME DON'TS

Don't Speak Too Much

If you find you are speaking more than your children, you are speaking too much. A conversation is not an opportunity for a lecture.

Don't Disagree Too Early

Explore why your child believes what he or she does. If you are going to have to genuinely disagree, you need to disagree in a way that keeps the channels of communication open. It is okay to disagree—after all, if your child says "stealing is fine because K-Mart isn't going to go broke if I rip them off," you cannot simply let them think that is okay. However, the hypothetical nature of the questions allows you to explore and break down your child's view. On the other hand, if the police bring your child home for having stolen something from K-Mart, feel free to make as many absolute pronouncements as you like.

Don't Set Yourself Up As The Final Answer

If someone told you that they were going to have an ethical discussion with you, but that they would be telling you the correct answer at the end, you probably wouldn't take the discussion seriously. Neither will your children.

CONVERSATIONS WITH THE ETHICALLY CHALLENGED CHILD

As I stated earlier, I do not believe that this book is merely a values clarification exercise. I believe that certain values are better than others: generosity is better than selfishness, kindness is better than cruelty. So what happens if a child says, "Well, actually, I don't mind if I rip people off and am mean to them, because my value is 'always look out for Number One.'" When faced with that statement, I don't believe it's okay to say, "Well in our relative twenty first century world, if it's fine for you darling, then it's fine with me, now onto the next question." I would rather you said, "That's appalling, you selfish beast, I can't believe you are my child." At least you would have made a moral stand. However, I also strongly believe that asking follow-up questions that pull apart their attitude will usually have much more long-term effect than dressing them down. Some (loaded) follow-up questions to the statement about ripping people off could include:

- universalizing it—"What if everyone acted like that? Would you really be able to get very far in life then?"

- implying a social contract—"You are relying on other people to trust you, even as you rip them off. Is this fair?"

- accepting the premise, but disputing the result—"You want to look out for number one, but is turning everyone else off you a good way of doing this or are your hurting your own reputation?"

If all else fails, I believe you would be within your rights to ultimately name the behavior and express disapproval: "I think that is selfish and I can't pretend that it's okay." The danger is that your child will then stop having ethics discussions with you at all. You'll have lost the chance for them to reflect on and perhaps change their ethical way of looking at things. It will depend on each situation and your own style of parenting. In addition, do remember that these conversations are hypothetical and your child may well be testing out different moral positions—don't immediately jump to one conclusion and see calamity.

GENERAL POINTS ABOUT USING THIS BOOK

- The book is written with a "target" age range of about ten to fifteen years. This is quite a range. I have included an Ⓜ rating against some of the topics. This could be because the concepts are a little bit tougher, because they explicitly deal with philosophers or because they involve some violent or challenging facts. It is up to you whether to deal with them— certainly it would be great if your children were up to it in one way or another.

- Some of the questions in the conversations are not there as reasonable positions (e.g. "Should children not have to do any housework at all?" "Is all tax just theft?"). Instead, they are there as extreme propositions to get a discussion going. Hopefully you will be able to spot these ones. Please don't think that just because something is written as a question that there are two equal sides.

- There is no such thing as a simple "yes/no" answer in this book. For example, "Is music piracy the same thing as stealing from a store?" does not expect a "yes" or "no." Instead it is a starting point to explore. If the questions in this book don't have a "why/why not?" at the end of them, you should usually add one.

- Some of the conversations in this book merely scratch the surface of an issue. A good example of this is behavior in cyberspace. Hopefully the ethics conversations in this book will open up a place for discussion with your children. There are many other books and websites that can explore issues more fully in almost every case

- Many of the questions are hypothetical. It is easy to try to get "around" hypotheticals. For example, "If there was one piece of chocolate left in the world, who would you share it with, your best friend or your sibling? Why?" In this case, many children will say, "I'd cut it into three pieces and share it with both." Although this is laudable, it also dodges the hard questions about how and why you value your friends and your family.

- Throughout I have used the terms "your father" or "your mother" in hypotheticals. I also write about big brothers, little sisters, aunts, etc. The alternative was to have the book littered with clunky sentences such as "Your primary caregiver asks you if you have cheated at school." I recognize that in many cases the use of specifics such as father, mother, aunt, will not be true for your family. I hope that you are able to see past this to the substance of the questions.

In any case, the first conversation now looms. . . I hope that you get a lot out of this book with your children and have a great time with the many vigorous discussions that follow. Enjoy!

1

MUSIC DOWNLOADS
AND STEALING

A. Do you think Casey has done anything wrong in the following situations?

i)   Casey loves music. He goes into a (foolish) CD store that has the CDs in the covers and takes half a dozen of them.

ii) Casey loves music. He borrows dozens of CDs off his friends and downloads them onto his iTunes.

iii) Casey loves music. He downloads five albums from a filesharing server such as limewire onto his iTunes.

iv) Casey loves music. He downloads five thousand albums from a filesharing server such as limewire onto his iTunes.

B. What would happen if everyone downloaded music for free from the internet?

C. Is music piracy from the internet for free the same thing as stealing from a store? What is different? What is the same?

D. Bob loves the computer game "Finland Invades!" in which Finnish armies draped in Finnish flags invade other countries and shoot local people. However, he is a proud American. He gets into the code of the program and changes it so that the soldiers look American instead of Finnish, and wear the American flag instead of the Finnish flag. He calls it "America invades!" and tries to sell it over the internet. Has Bob done anything wrong?

STEALING???

Are the following situations stealing?

A. In English class Matthew borrows a pen from Brett's pencil case without telling Brett.

    i) At the end of the period he puts it back in Brett's pencil case.

    ii) At the end of the period he forgets to put it back.

    iii) At the end of the period he decides he quite likes it and will keep it for the rest of the week.

B. Brett is sick of Matthew taking his pens from his pencil case. At the end of recess, he takes Matthew's bag and dumps it on the other side of the school.

C. Chloe has not done her English assignment. Her friend Sasha has. Chloe takes the assignment from Sasha's bag and copies it without telling Sasha, changing a few words here and there. She then puts it back in Sasha's bag.

D. Joe has not done his English assignment. His friend Felix has. Joe asks Felix if he can copy the assignment and Felix agrees. Joe copies it.

E. Phoebe starts up a company offering "safe and sound investment options for retired people." Old Man Scott gives Phoebe all of his retirement money. Phoebe invests in very risky companies on the stock exchange. All of these companies go broke. Phoebe loses all of Scott's money.

F. John makes $100,000 per year. The government takes $20,000 of it to pay for hospitals, school, education, and other necessities.

G. What is the difference between "stealing" and "sharing?"

H. What would a society be like in which everyone stole? What would it be like for you?

I. What would stop you from stealing $100 from the wallet of someone else in your class?

STUCK ON A LIFEBOAT

The cruise liner you were on has sunk and you are now on a lifeboat with some other passengers. The lifeboat has been bobbing on the ocean for a week and you ran out of food two days ago. You are about to run out of water too. There is a good chance that a boat might come and pick you up, but there is also a good chance that you will be stuck on the lifeboat until. . . the end. Mrs. Jones takes charge of the lifeboat and starts to force the other survivors to make choices. What do you do in the following situations?

A. She says that it is quite likely people will die, and everyone has to take a vote as to whether they will start eating the survivors. Eating the survivors will extend your life by a week or two. Do you vote to start culling the people in the lifeboat?

B. The vote to eat the other survivors was successful. Now you have to decide who gets eaten. Mrs. Jones says that you can either put everyone's name in a cap and draw each out randomly, or choose by deciding which people are most worth saving. Do you vote to decide randomly, or do you decide by looking at what each person is worth?

C. The boat decides to choose randomly. Then Mrs. Jones reveals that one passenger is a serial killer, while another passenger is a doctor on the brink of discovering the cure for cancer. She asks you to vote again. Do you vote for random selection, or by looking at people's worth?

D. This time, the boat decides to eat people on the basis of their worth. Mrs. Jones insists that everyone has to rank the people from one to eight, from the first to be eaten to the last to be eaten. The eight people are:

i)   You

ii) Mrs. Irina Jones—Headmistress of a school

iii) Mr. Bob Pratchett—doctor, about to discover cure for cancer

iv) Mr. Felonious Spike—serial killer and bank robber

v)   Mrs. Rani Chandra—member of the government in Fiji and mother of three children

vi) Nelson Po—two-year-old child

vii) Mr. David Spicer—seventy- five-year-old family man and former train driver

viii) Felicity Lamond—twenty-five-year-old lawyer for a big tobacco company, single, and ten weeks pregnant

In what order do you eat the survivors?

IS STEALING
EVER OKAY?

Do you think any of the following examples of stealing would be okay? Why?

A. Robin lives in a forest. When BMWs and Mercedes drive down the forest road he holds them up and takes all the owners' valuables. He donates all of this money to The Red Cross.

B. Marion works for a bank. She inserts a program into the bank's computer that takes five cents per month out of every single bank account and reroutes it to charity. No customer notices this money missing.

C. John works in a bank. His mother is very sick. His children are comfortable but not wealthy. John is in charge of the account of Skug Skunkley, a notorious mafia boss, murderer, and underworld figure. Skug has never earned an honest cent in his life and spends most of his money on drugs, liquor, and fast cars. John takes $100,000 from Skug's account and spends it on hospital care for his mother and an overseas trip for his children.

D. Tuck works for the American Diplomatic Service. He copies all of their secret papers onto a USB and smuggles them out. He gives them all to Julian who publishes them on the internet.

E. The British Museum has on display in London some aboriginal spears that were taken in 1839. The Noongar people of Western Australia tell the Museum that these spears are sacred items from their tribe. The British Museum ignores them. A crack squad of Noongar hitmen then break into the Museum one night and take the spears. They also take a British diamond-studded religious cup that was made in 1839.

ETHICAL THINKER— PLATO

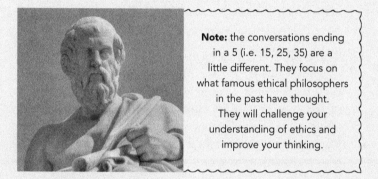

Note: the conversations ending in a 5 (i.e. 15, 25, 35) are a little different. They focus on what famous ethical philosophers in the past have thought. They will challenge your understanding of ethics and improve your thinking.

A. **Plato** felt that the human soul was broken up into three parts. He compared these three parts to an insect with a head, a chest, and an abdomen.

Head = reason and wisdom (if you're lucky)

Chest = emotion, courage

Abdomen = appetite

i) What would happen if you made ethical decisions (e.g. about whether to execute a murderer)?

 • only with your head (rationality)?

- only with your chest (emotion)?

- only with your abdomen (appetite)?

ii) If you could *only* have one of the three parts (head, chest, or abdomen) when making ethical decisions, which one would you choose?

Plato believed that reason and rationality were the most important things when deciding what was ethical—certainly more important than the *experience* of living. So, for example, someone's view about euthanasia should be based on rationality, not their reactions to a sick family member.

B. Plato had a number of ideas about how to govern a state ethically and well. What do you think about each of them? Do you think they are good ideas? Would they work well in our society?

i) The state should be ruled by philosophers because they will be trained to be the most intelligent and rational people.

ii) The rulers of the state should not be allowed to have possessions or families, because these will distract the rulers from doing their job justly.

iii) Women can rule as well as men, but should not have to do any childrearing or housekeeping.

iv) Children are too important to be left to their families and should mainly be brought up by the state (in nurseries and schools).

6

WHAT IS CHEATING AT SCHOOL?

A. Is copying out of the back of a math textbook cheating? Why?

B. Is copying your friend's work before school starts one morning cheating? Why?

C. Is using your friend's work as a base for your own work cheating? Why?

D. Is cutting and pasting from the internet cheating? Why?

E. Would it be cheating if every single person on the class agreed to pass around the answers of the best person in the class?

F. You copy off the person in front of you in a test, but the person in front of you gets the answer wrong. Is this cheating?

G. You notice the person behind you trying to copy your answers. You are offended by this. Is it okay to write down the wrong answers on purpose, and then change them later?

H. What do you think cheating is?

I. What do you think plagiarism is?

J. Would it be okay for only you to cheat and no- one else?

K. What would society be like if everyone cheated? Describe what it would be like at:

  i)   school

  ii) work

  iii) home

7

S P O R T S

A. If you are playing tennis and you hit the ball "out" but the other player thinks it was "in," should you insist that it was out?

B. If you are playing hockey, should you "accidentally" hit other players in the shins with your hockey stick? What if the other team starts doing it to members of your team?

C. Should you argue with a referee if you think there is a 50/50 chance that the referee got it wrong?

D. If your mother or father keeps shouting at the referee, "Open your eyes ref!" should they stop? Should you tell them to be quiet?

E. If you commit a "travel" in basketball, the referee doesn't notice it, you score off it and win the game, is this cheating?

F. Is taking protein powders cheating? Why?

G. Is taking anabolic steroids cheating? Why? Is there a difference between these and protein powders?

H. If you are a professional baseball team and you disagree with the rules about the salary cap (i.e. each club can't pay more than a certain amount of money to people in the team), should you obey them or should you not? Why?

KILLING A MADMAN

Imagine that you have just invented a time machine. It is a rickety piece made up of bicycle parts and held together with violin strings, but it does travel through time. However, it only carries one person at a time. You hop into it and pull the lever that says "Past." The scene around you blurs and fades and things start to go backwards. Before long everything outside your machine is just a blur. Your time monitor is clicking past the numbers now... 1980, 1950, 1910. . . faster and faster.

At 1895 your machine splutters and coughs, and some of the violin strings snap. There is a billowing of smoke, and your machine finally crash lands in 1889. You get out of the machine. You are in a cute looking nursery in what seems to be a middle European country such as Austria. You look out the window and you are five floors up. You see a bassinette and can hear the sound of a baby inside it.

You go over and inside is a little baby boy. You then look at the back of the bassinette and see the baby's name tag. It says *Adolf Hitler*, the name of the man who killed millions of people by starting World War II and ordered the deaths of millions more in concentration camps. You look into the baby's face and know instinctively it is him.

You can hear footsteps coming up the stairs.

You can't put the baby in the machine with you (it only carries one person at a time). If you are found in the room in 20 seconds time you will be arrested.

You can't come back to this room as the time machine is not reliable enough.

A. Do you throw the little Adolf Hitler out of the window and jump back into the machine?

B. What do you think about the baby Hitler?

    i) Was he already evil? Was he "born" evil?

    ii) If he became "evil" later, what would make him evil?

    iii) Is it okay to "punish" him for something he has not yet done?

(G-RATED) PARTIES

A. Your best friend invites you to his birthday party. His parents are against party food and only serve fruit. The main event at the party will be watching a video you have already seen three times. Someone else from your class who you hardly know invites you to an amazing bowling party that lots of your friends will be going to. What do you do and why?

B. You are in a gang of ten, which includes Maria and Sharon. Maria has a party and invites nine of the gang along. She does not include Sharon, because she says she is "sick" of Sharon. Sharon is very hurt but won't say anything to Maria. Do you just let it ride (it's Maria's party after all) or do you try to get her to invite Sharon?

C. Your friend bought you a $10 present when they came to your party last month. Your mother says you can spend one of three amounts on your friend:

i) $2

ii) $10

iii) $100

Which one do you spend and why?

D. You go to a good friend's birthday party and it is very, very boring. The music is terrible and all the food is made of soy beans. Within an hour other friends of yours are leaving. Do you stay for your friend, or do you get out of there with some of the others?

E. You go to a good friend's birthday party. It turns out that some cousins of his have brought firecrackers to the party and turned them into small bombs. They and your good friend decide to go out and blow up some mailboxes. You think this is a terrible idea. Your friend says to you "Oh come on buddy, this is my birthday. Coming would be like a big birthday present to me." Do you go along or do you go home?

CONVERSATION 10

BEING RECIPROCAL

Note: the conversations ending in a 0 (i.e. 10, 20, 30) are a little different. They focus on HOW to think ethically. They are about developing thinking skills. They will sharpen your mind and improve your cognitive capabilities.

Brief explanation: Being reciprocal means you believe it is okay to do something because you had it done to you. It also may make you feel like you owe something to other people. Being reciprocal may work in some situations and not others. The following examples will help you to work out when being reciprocal is a useful ethical tool and when it is not.

Should you be reciprocal in the following situations?

A. Steve gave you a chip. You should give Steve a piece of gum.

B. Steve hit you. It is okay to hit Steve.

C. Steve shot your father. It is justifiable to shoot Steve's father.

D. Steve lent you $10 last month. You should lend Steve $10 this month.

E. Steve visited you when you were in the hospital. You should visit Steve when he is in the hospital.

F. Steve never pays you or your family what he owes you. You should never pay Steve or his family what you owe them.

G. Steve used an illegal program to download all of his iTunes library into yours. You should use the same program to download your iTunes library into Steve's.

H. Steve stole your bus pass. It is okay to steal Steve's bus pass.

GENDER RELATIONS

A. Do guys rate girls? Do girls rate guys? Is this fair? Should it be done?

B. If you had a sister/brother, how would you expect her/him to be treated by the opposite sex at a party? How do you treat the opposite sex at a party?

C. Do the guys/girls you see on music videos and television affect the way you see guys/girls in real life? If so, in what way? Is this fair? Does it matter?

D. How are members of the opposite sex different to you? How are they similar to you?

E. Do girls and guys "dumb themselves down" when speaking to each other? If so, why? Is this a good thing? If it is not a good thing, how could it change?

F. What happens if a boy/girl drinks alcohol at a party? How does someone's behavior change if they drink alcohol? Do people find this more or less attractive?

G. How do girls and guys act differently in cyberspace? Why do you think this happens? What does everyone need to be careful of in cyberspace?

12

WORLD OF LIARS

A. Imagine a society where there are lies everywhere.

    i)   Imagine you go to a shoe store and pick out a pair of sneakers for $100. You take them to the register and the sales assistant charges you $200. You protest, and she replies "Oh, the price tag was a lie to make you want to buy the sneakers." Is this acceptable or effective? Why?

    ii)   Imagine your math teacher sets a test for Friday. On Thursday she gives you the test. When you protest she says "Oh, Friday was a lie so I could see who studied for the test well in advance." Is this acceptable? Why?

B. Imagine your parents tell you that you can have $10 for cleaning the house. After you have cleaned it they tell you it was just a lie to get you to clean up.

i) How would you feel about living in a society where people lied like this all the time?

ii) What is wrong with it?

iii) What would you start doing?

iv) Would this society work?

v) Would you want to live there?

vi) If you don't like being lied to, do you have an obligation to tell the truth?

C. Can lies ever be good?

i) Imagine you go to a shoe store and pick out a pair of sneakers for $100. You take them to the register and the sales assistant charges you $80. You point out the difference, and she replies, "Oh, we have a sale, but we are not going to put up signs or change the price tags." Is this acceptable or effective?

ii) Imagine your math teacher sets a test for Thursday. You don't study. On Thursday she tells you the test is on Friday. When you ask why she says "Oh, I always thought I would give you an extra day to study." Is this acceptable?

WHAT MAKES A LIE?

Do you think that the following situations are lies? If they are, are they okay?

A. You are in a market in Turkey. You want to buy a rug. A shop-keeper tells you that his lowest price is $1000. You say you cannot possibly afford more than $800. After some more haggling, you agree on $900 as a price.

B. A real estate agent tells possible buyers that a house will sell at auction for $800,000. Although he can't *know*, he thinks that the house will probably sell for a million dollars.

C. Fred Smith is in Congress. He believes strongly that the speed limit should be 60 mph. His political party's leader proposes a law that the new speed limit should be 40 mph. When it comes to a vote, Fred Smith votes with the rest of his party to lower the speed limit.

D. You are fairly sure that your friends are planning to shoplift shoes from a store at the local shopping center. However, each time they start planning it, you put your hands over your ears and walk away. Your parents ask you about rumors that people are planning to steal from the shop. You tell them that you know nothing about it.

E. You eat all of your mother's favorite chocolates at 12:30 A.M. on Monday morning. Your father says to you on Wednesday, "Did you eat my chocolates over the weekend?" You say "No."

F. A scientist is 80% sure that her research shows that her new drug will cure cancer. She claims that she is absolutely sure that this new drug will cure cancer.

IS IT EVER OKAY
TO LIE?

Do you think it would be okay to lie in the following situations? Why/why not?

A. Your grandmother knits you a sweater for Christmas. It is ugly and uncomfortable. When she asks what you think of it, you tell her it is really nice.

B. You begin work at a sports store. Your employer takes you to a pile of shoes with price tags of $100. He tells you to take off the tags, and replace them with tags that reads "SALE! 50% OFF!! WERE $200, NOW $100." You tell him that this is a lie. The manager tells you to get on with it, or you'll lose your job.

C. In a case of mistaken identity, the Mafia come to school to kill your friend Steve. You are in a classroom on the ground floor of a building. Steve goes to the classroom next door to hide. The Mafia politely ask you where Steve is. You tell them he has gone up to the next floor.

D. Your friend Bob smokes marijuana at home and has tried to get you to join in.

　　i)　Your friend Dave asks you if Bob smokes marijuana. You say "No."

　　ii)　Your parents ask you if Bob smokes marijuana. You say "No".

iii) Bob's parents ask you if Bob smokes marijuana. You say "No."

iv) The Principal asks you if Bob smokes marijuana. You say "No."

v) The police ask you if Bob smokes marijuana. You say "No."

vi) A new drug dealer asks you if Bob smokes marijuana. You say "No."

E. Your little sister's pet canary Tweetie dies. She is very sad. But, through her tears, she tells you it has gone to bird paradise where the sky is glorious pink, the trees grow birdseed fruit, and all birds fly together in avian harmony. She asks you if you believe in bird paradise. You tell her that you do.

F. America is successfully invaded by Canada. You have fields on the right and left of your house. A local resistance group plants landmines on the field to the right of your house. The Canadian army comes by and asks you which field has landmines in it. You fake a Canadian accent and tell them that it is the field to the left. The army then travels through the field on the right and is blown up by landmines.

What are the differences between the situations when it may have been okay to lie and situations when it wasn't?

ETHICAL THINKER — ARISTOTLE

> **Note:** the conversations ending in a 5 (i.e. 15, 25, 35) are a little different. They focus on what famous ethical philosophers in the past have thought. They will challenge your understanding of ethics and improve your thinking.

A. **Aristotle** was the opposite of Plato (Conversation 5). He believed, broadly, that what people learned from their life experience should guide their ethical decisions.

What do you think should guide your ethical decisions—your rationality, or your life experience? The following examples may help you discuss:

i) Should you give 90% of your family's money to famine relief?

ii) Should you beat up someone who hurt your sister?

iii) Should you become a vegetarian (if you are not one already)?

B. Aristotle believed that there were three types of happiness:

- pleasure

- life as a free and responsible citizen

- life as a thinker and philosopher

Which one do you think is the most important? If one of the following three things had to happen to you, which one would you choose and why?

i) You lose almost all of your material possessions (without any chance of getting them back).

ii) America becomes a terrible dictatorship and all freedoms are suspended (e.g. freedom of speech, freedom to vote).

iii) You are in a car accident and lose your ability to think about more than basic things.

C. Aristotle thought your character was made up of a series of elements (e.g. how *confident* you were). He felt that if you had too much or too little of these character traits that would be bad (e.g. if you are too confident you are reckless and if you are not confident enough you are a coward). However, if you had a golden mean of these elements then you would be good and virtuous (e.g. just enough confidence makes you courageous).

See if you can work out what would happen if people got too much or too little of each of the following character traits:

	JUST RIGHT	TOO MUCH	TOO LITTLE
Getting and giving money	Generous	Wasteful	?
Anger	Gentle	?	Spiritless
Pleasant in life	Friendly	Crawler	?
Truth about self	Knows truth	Boastful	?

16

MORE LIES!!

A. Is there any such thing as a "white lie?" Is a "white lie" okay or not okay? Can you create a test to tell the difference between "ethical" and "unethical" white lies?

B. Imagine a society where everyone told the truth all the time. What would it be like? Would there be anything wrong about living there?

C. Try to remember a situation where someone lied to you. How did you feel? What do you think that person *should* have done?

D. Telling a lie is not illegal. Should it be?

E. What harm does lying do:

    i)   to the person being lied to?

    ii) to the liar?

    iii) to society?

F. If *everyone* in society lied, would it become an ethical thing?

G. If someone has lied to you is it okay to lie back to them?

17

MONEY,
MONEY, MONEY, AND
INHERITANCE

(Justice Between the Generations)

A. If your parents earn a lot of money, should they have to save some of it for you or can they spend it all?

B. If you earn a lot of money, should you have to save some it for your children, or can you spend it all?

C. If your great aunt Mildred leaves you five million dollars, can you spend it all? Or should you leave a lot of it for your great nephews and nieces?

D. If your great aunt Mildred left your parents five million dollars, should they keep some of it for you?

E. Your parents looked after you when you were very young. Are you obliged to look after them when they are very old?

ALCOHOL

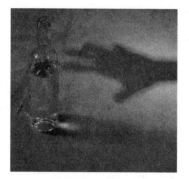

A. Should the legal drinking age be lowered to 18 or 16 or 12? Why/why not?

B. Should alcohol be made illegal for all people? Why/why not?

C. Why is drinking alcohol legal for adults but not for teenagers?

D. Is it hypocritical of an adult to tell a teenager not to drink, and then drink themselves?

E. If someone does not agree with the law in a country about the legal drinking age, should they break it? Why or why not?

F. Studies have shown that alcohol has a bad effect on the developing teenage brain. Does this mean that it is wrong for teenagers to drink?

G. If a person gets drunk and does the following things, was the drinking morally wrong?

i) Has a headache in the morning

ii) Assaults someone at a party

iii) Smiles at people at a party and falls asleep

iv) Reveals someone's most embarrassing secret at a party

v) Has to go to hospital and get his/her stomach pumped at the cost of many thousands of dollars

vi) Gets alcohol poisoning and dies

vii) Ruins his own liver (over many decades) and dies

viii) In the cases above, were the *acts* unethical or the *drinking* unethical? Or neither?

ix) Is being drunk morally wrong if you don't know which of the above acts are going to happen?

x) If you had to make up the laws about drinking alcohol in the U.S.A., what would they be?

19

SMOKING

A. Why do adults smoke?

B. Why do teenagers smoke?

C. Smoking can kill you. Is it unethical to do something that will probably kill you over a long period of time?

D. For teenagers, dying at 60 sounds like 'dying when you are old.' For adults, dying at 60 sounds like 'dying when you are young.' Smoking makes you die younger.

    i)   Is it unethical for adults to let teenagers start something that will probably reduce their lifespan?

    ii)   Is it unethical for adults to interfere in a teenager's own decision?

E. Should smoking cigarettes be made illegal? Why/why not?

F. Cigarette companies know that smoking is addictive and kills you. Should they be closed down and their directors charged with manslaughter?

G. Airplane companies know that some of their planes crash and people die. Should they be closed down and their directors charged with manslaughter? What is the difference between and airplane company and a cigarette company?

H. Are people entitled to do stupid things? If people want to smoke, should cigarette companies be allowed to make them cigarettes?

CONVERSATION

20

USING CRITERIA

Criteria are guidelines that we can use to judge things for ourselves. For example if we wanted to judge whether we should buy a pair of sneakers, we would use criteria such as price, style, and quality.

Criteria can make us judge ethical decisions one way or another. For example, a sheriff in a Wild West town might decide whether to execute a outlaw, or keep him in jail. If he used the criteria of "cost," then he would execute the robber (saving the cost of meals, cleaning, guards, etc.) If he used the criteria of "mercy," he would not execute the robber. Using different criteria can result in completely different ethical decisions. So we need to know when we are using them.

A. Imagine that an asteroid hits your school one day when you are at home sick, and obliterates it. You have to pick a new school and you are allowed to visit five. You can go anywhere you like. Think up a list of what things you will be looking for when you go to each of the schools. This list will help you ask questions and make decisions. This is a criteria list that you will use to rank the schools.

CONVERSATION 21

DEATH AND TAXES

A. Imagine that you do not earn very much money and you have three children to support. At the same time Jim earns a LOT of money and also has three children. Indeed, he has enough for them each to buy a really nice house with his money when he dies. Should the government tax Jim when he dies to the extent that his children do not have as big an advantage over your children?

B. Imagine that you earn millions and millions of dollars in your life. Enough for each of your children to have a really nice house without paying a cent of their own. On the other hand, Jim earns practically nothing and has no money for his children. Should the government tax you when you die so that your children do not get as much of an advantage over Jim's children?

C. Should a *nation* (e.g. America) pay people who were wronged by a previous generation (e.g. Native Americans, African Americans) using money accumulated by the taxation system? Why/why not?

RANK THE CRIMINALS

You live in a country called Atopia, which is very similar to ours. One difference is that they have a court system in which one judge decides whether people are guilty, and then a different judge decides what sentence the guilty people will receive.

You have become one of the sentencing judges. Eight criminals have come before you for sentencing and you have to decide how to sentence them.

The rules of the sentencing court are:

- Guilty parties come before you in batches of eight.
- One person in each batch must be hanged.
- One person in each batch must receive a suspended sentence (i.e. no jail time).
- The other six people need to have 40 years of jail distributed amongst them in any proportion you see fit (shortest: one week, longest, 39 years and 47 weeks).

A. Who do you hang?

B. Who do you set free?

C. How much jail time do you give the other six?

> **Note:** a good way to do this is to rank the eight criminals and then decide how much jail time to give the middle six.

The eight criminals who have been sent to you for sentencing are:

- **Bob** has been taking drugs for five years. (In that time he has had several jobs as a bricklayer, courier, and bartender.) One night, while high on drugs and low on money, he bashed a random man coming out of a bar in order to steal his wallet. This included breaking the man's jaw, and then stomping his head while he was on the ground. The man now has minor brain damage and is partially paralyzed on one side.

- **Larry** was a National Court Judge, President of the Atopian Human Rights Association, and a highly respected national figure. He was photographed going through three sets of red lights. Each time he did it he got other people to swear on affidavits that they were driving his car. Larry was charged with making a false statement. When the case came to court, he continued to swear on oath that he was not driving the car. Undeniable proof was produced showing that he did. He has been convicted of "perjury"— lying to the court.

- **Maria** is the Managing Director of a major oil company. Several reports were shown to her demonstrating that her oil rig off the coast of Atopia was dangerous and unsafe. She did nothing about it. When her Field Operations Manager told her she needed to make the rigs safer she had him moved to another job. The oil rig blew up, killing 13 people and sending millions of barrels of oil washing up on the Atopian coastline, devastating the local industry.

- **Shelley** is a mother whose teenage daughter was being bullied by another girl named Chloe. Shelley went onto Facebook pretending to be a teenage boy, and had an online "relationship" with Chloe. Shelley then broke the "relationship" off, was extremely offensive to Chloe, and told Chloe that she should go and kill herself. Chloe killed herself.

- **Larissa** found herself short of money. She used a gun to rob a bank and escaped with $200,000.

- **Enrique** set up a company that "sold" a special fuel which made gas 20% more efficient. He encouraged people to invest in it. Hundreds of people did, some of them using their life's savings. There was no such fuel and Enrique knew it. Enrique lived well for five years, sponsoring basketball teams and spending lavishly. Eventually the company collapsed, leaving no money or assets. Dozens of people were financially ruined.

- **Melissa** was physically abused by her husband for ten years and sustained significant injuries. She regularly reported it to the police, but nothing happened. One evening she hid behind the front door and stabbed him to death as he walked in the door.

- **John** went on a cruise where he spiked Felicity's drink with a drug that made her feel more uninhibited. She was not aware of this. They slept together. Felicity then went to sleep in another bed in the cabin. In the morning he could not wake her, so he left her in the bed and went out. She had a bad reaction to the drug and died in her bed at 11:00 A.M.

OUR GRANDCHILDREN
AND THE PLANET

Note: This discussion follows statements made by the overwhelming majority of climate scientists that the earth is warming partly due to human activity. It also has as its starting point the information that there is a high probability of temperature rises of at least 2 degrees by 2100, with various predictable and unpredictable results.

A. The use of carbon-based products contributes (with more than 95% probability) to heating up the atmosphere. When deciding what to do about climate change how much should we consider :

i) us?

ii) our grandchildren?

iii) our great, great, great, great, great, great, great, grandchildren?

When thinking about future generations, what should we do about climate change?

B. Coal is due to run out in the next few centuries. Should we use coal much more slowly?

C. Should we continue to use energy at a high rate and rely on either scientists inventing something or politicians doing something to stop the earth heating up? Or should we cut our own use of energy by up to 80%? What might cutting our own use of energy by 80% look like?

D. The Amazon rainforest is largely in the country of Brazil. Imagine that the Amazon rainforest could be all cut down and farmed without any impact on climate change. Could Brazil cut it all down, or do they have an obligation to future generations who may want to see it? Do they have other obligations?

RIGHTS OF
ANIMALS

A. Imagine that a *vastly* superior (and culinary) alien race comes down to Earth and contacts you as the ambassador.

"We are planning to hunt and eat ten million people a year," they tell you politely, with saliva dripping from the sides of their mouths. "We hope you don't mind."

"That's unfair," you reply, with feeling.

They look confused. "But we don't understand," they say. "Your species eats all sorts of animals. We are so much smarter than you, it makes the difference between you and a cow seems like nothing. Why can't we eat you?"

What do you tell them? What arguments do you present for why you shouldn't be eaten?

B. What are the similarities between humans and other "higher order" mammals?

C. What are the differences between humans and other "higher order" mammals?

D. Animals are often regarded as less intelligent or moral than humans. Does this mean that we have the right to eat them?

E. People in comas are often regarded as less intelligent or moral that other humans. Does this mean we have the right to eat them?

ETHICAL THINKERS—
HOBBES AND LOCKE

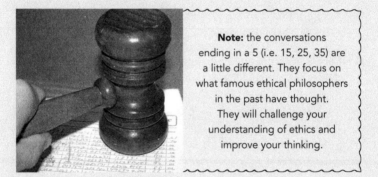

Note: the conversations ending in a 5 (i.e. 15, 25, 35) are a little different. They focus on what famous ethical philosophers in the past have thought. They will challenge your understanding of ethics and improve your thinking.

Thomas Hobbes held that people originally lived in a state of nature that was anarchic. When people came to live in societies they gave up some of their freedom to do whatever they wanted in return for protection. This "deal" with society he called the social contract. He called the state they lived in the Leviathan. He felt that you should never break the social contract by going against the state's laws.

John Locke agreed with many of Hobbes' ideas about the social contract. However, he said that if the leader of the state was making completely unjust laws, then the social contract was broken. If this happened, people could break the laws and rise up against the leader.

A. Who do you agree with, Hobbes or Locke? What would happen if no one ever broke a law, no matter how unjust? What would happen if people felt they could break any law that they didn't agree with?

B. Below are a number of rules you might feel are not good. Which ones, if any, would you break?

    i)   The speed limit is 60 mph on a road and you think it should be 70 mph.

    ii)   Black people have to sit on the back of the bus and white people should not sit at the back with them (this was law in the U.S.A. until the 1960s).

    iii) People cannot buy alcohol until they are 18 years of age.

    iv) Companies cannot employ people under the age of 13 years of age.

    v)   You can't throw paint on the president when he/she comes to visit your town.

    vi) More than eight people cannot gather together in one place. If they do, the army is allowed to come and arrest them.

SHOULD WE EAT MEAT?

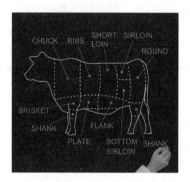

A. What are the arguments for and against eating the following animals:

i) an oyster?

ii) an old chicken?

iii) a sheep?

iv) a lamb?

v) a whale?

vi) a human?

B. If you are drawing a line somewhere (i.e. you say it is okay to eat an old chicken, but not a lamb), how are you drawing this line? Can you justify this line?

C. Is "eating meat" a human need or a human want? What would happen if no one ate meat?

D. Why do people actually eat meat? How moral are these reasons?

SHOULD WE USE ANIMAL PRODUCTS?

A. Is it okay to keep an animal in a farm and use the following products from it:

i) its wool to wear?

ii) its eggs to eat?

iii) its milk to drink?

iv) its offspring to eat?

B. Should we use the term "its" or "her" when referring to an animal? Should we use the term "children" to refer to its offspring? Do these things make a difference in your answer?

C. Should animals be used for testing in laboratories in the following ways:

- For medicinal cures and the treatment is painful?

- For cosmetic products and the treatment is painful?

- For medicinal cures and the treatment is very unlikely to be painful?

- For cosmetic products and the treatment is very unlikely to be painful?

KILLING ANIMALS

A. In order for us to eat meat, animals need to be killed. Is it important to kill animals "humanely" and is there any such thing?

   i) Should they be stunned before they are killed?

   ii) Should they be kept unaware that other animals are being killed?

   iii) Should we send animals overseas to be slaughtered? Are we responsible for the treatment of the animals once they are overseas?

B. Does killing an animal "humanely" mean that it is morally okay to raise and kill an animal for food?

C. Should there be a minimum age at which we can kill animals?

D. Does it make a moral difference whether a chicken is "free range" or kept in a cage? Why?

E. Does it make a moral difference whether a pig is kept in a pen or in a more "free range" environment?

F. Is it better to raise something to kill it (e.g. a cow) or hunt and/or fish something from the wild (e.g. a salmon)?

G. Would it be okay to go hunting squirrels for sport if they were over-running an area? Would it be okay to go hunting wild pigs for sport in the same area?

H. Would it be okay to go hunting an animal for sport that was not a pest but neither was it endangered?

I. Imagine that you lived in India. Would it be okay to kill a tiger at the edge of a National Forest that had been attacking and killing villagers in the outlying fields? What if the tiger was endangered?

29

SHOULD WE CAGE ANIMALS?

A. Should dogs and cats be kept as pets?

B. Should a dog have a yard big enough to run around in, or is it okay to be kept in a small yard and taken for walks?

C. Should birds be kept in cages that do not allow them to fly?

D. Should fish be kept in a goldfish bowl that is too small?

E. Is it hypocritical to keep a pet rabbit and love it, and then to eat a chicken for dinner?

F. Should small animals such as monkeys and dogs be kept in circuses and taught tricks?

G. Should larger animals such as tigers and elephants be kept in circuses and taught tricks?

H. Are circus animals pets of the owners, or something else?

I. Some people believe that zoos are unfair on animals. Do you agree or disagree with them? When could a zoo be unfair? When could it be fair?

J. If an animal had lived in a zoo/cage/circus for all of its life, would it be fair to release it into the wild?

WHAT IS A FACT?
WHAT IS AN OPINION?

Note: the conversations ending in a 0 (i.e. 10, 20, 30) are a little different. They focus on HOW to think ethically. They are about developing thinking skills. They will sharpen your mind and improve your cognitive capabilities.

There are different types of opinions:

- **Opinion of preference**
  e.g. "I like nachos more than I like chips."

  You don't need to show evidence or criteria with this type of opinion: it just expresses what you like.

- **Opinion of evaluation**
  e.g. "I think the president of America is doing a good job."

  With an opinion such us this, you need to show reasons and evidence for your view.

- **Opinion about a fact**
  e.g.: "Jenny Smith killed Joe Bloggs."

  Imagine that this is a murder trial in which Jenny Smith claims she is innocent and wasn't even there. There will be all sorts of evidence, heated arguments, and opinions given in the courtroom about whether the accusation is true or not. Evidence might point either way. If the case is reported in the media, everyone will have an opinion which will be argued in homes everywhere. However, the fact is either she did kill him or she didn't. Thus people's opinions are not opinions of preference or evaluation, but opinions about a fact.

Are the following facts or opinions? If they are opinions, what type are they?

i) Peach pie is better than pecan pie.

ii) Our school's soccer team is better than the opposition's soccer team.

iii) My parents are usually right.

iv) I should give my lunch money to help with the problem of famine in Africa.

v) World War II happened.

vi) The Battle of Hastings happened.

vii) Noah and the Flood happened.

viii) You should not take your phone to class if the school says you shouldn't.

ix) We should move drowning people's faces out of puddles.

x) We should lessen the amount of carbon dioxide in the air.

xi) Humans evolved from more simple animals.

31

SHOULD WE ACCEPT  ASYLUM SEEKERS?

A. When should a country such as America accept someone as a refugee?

i) Never..

ii) When the person's life is in danger because they have tried to get involved in politics/freedom of speech, etc.

iii) When their life is in danger because they belong to an ethnic or religious group that is being persecuted.

iv) When their life is in danger because the government in their country has broken down.

v) When they face a life of poverty and hardship because their country is impoverished.

vi) When they have a difficult life in their home country and they manage to make it to America.

B. How does a country such as America work out whether an asylum seeker was at risk of being killed in their former country?

C. What is a country's ethical responsibility to people originally outside its borders?

i) What if a hundred people in a boat arrive at New York City?

ii) What if there are one billion people in the world living below the basest poverty line?

D. Should America attempt to stop the "industry" of people smuggling? Why?

E. Is there a difference between people smugglers who make profit out of putting refugees on boats now and people smugglers who made profit out of putting Jewish people on boats in the 1930s?

F. Is there a difference between an asylum seeker in a refugee camp on the border between Afghanistan and Pakistan, and an asylum seeker who has made it to American territorial waters?

G. If you lived in a country where you were at risk of being killed for your religion, would you consider fleeing to a different country? What if you had children of your own—would you take them?

H. Elsewhere in this book, a number of ethical ideas are described (Conversations 45, 65, 75, 85). If you have already read them, try to link the theories to the problem of asylum seekers.

BAD CONSEQUENCES, RIGHT ACT?

A. Look at the following situations where acts that you take have bad results. Could any of these acts still be ethical acts?

i) You discover that your best friend is smoking marijuana in the evening. You are very worried about his health. He tells you that if you let his parents or the school know he will leave home and go and live with some friends in a bad part of town. These friends smoke pot three times every day. He says he has already got the money saved to do this. You tell his parents about his habit and he runs away.

ii) Your hockey team wins the local competition. You find out that three of the parents of people on your team bribed each of the referees. This made the difference between winning and losing in several games. You report them to your coach or the people who run the hockey competition and thus lose the competition.

B. Look at the following situations where acts that you take have good results. Could any of these acts still be unethical acts?

i) You stumble upon a bank account with $10,000 in it. It turns out to be a forgotten bank account of the dictator Muammar Gaddafi that he will never trace. You split the money among your five best friends.

ii) Your little sister's rabbit, Faffles, dies when she is away at school camp (through no fault of yours). You find an identical bunny at the local pet shop, put it in the hutch, and pretend it is Faffles.

C. Do you think an act can be judged good or bad depending on its results (its consequences)?

33

WHAT IS TORTURE?

> **Note:** This discussion should not be explored with children whose parents feel they may not be ready for it.

A. The World Medical Association in 1975 defined torture as "the deliberate, systematic, or wanton infliction of physical or mental suffering by one or more persons acting alone or on the orders of any authority, to force another person to yield information, to make a confession, or for any other reason." The United Nations definition adds that the pain has to be "severe" before it is torture. Do you believe the pain has to be "severe" for an act to be torture, or is "physical or mental suffering" enough?

B. Would you consider the following acts committed by an interrogator in a jail cell to be torture?

i) Dripping water on someone's forehead every five seconds for a day.

ii) Slapping someone on the face.

iii) Sticking someone's head in a bucket of water repeatedly.

iv) Telling someone their family will not be safe.

v) Telling someone their family will be kidnapped and murdered.

vi) Getting ten prisoners to pose in a line with dog collars on for photos.

vii) Putting someone in a room and forcing them to watch other people being tortured in the next room. Telling the person that if he "confesses" the other people will stop being tortured. However, the other people are all actors pretending to be tortured.

viii) Putting someone in a crowded jail cell for weeks.

IS TORTURE EVER 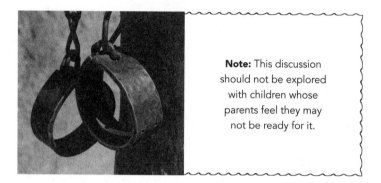 OKAY?

Note: This discussion should not be explored with children whose parents feel they may not be ready for it.

You are a member of the FBI. You have uncovered evidence of a bomb that will be carried onto a bus somewhere in your town this afternoon. It will kill dozens of people. (If you stop all of the buses, the bomber will walk into a building and detonate the bomb there, resulting in equal loss of life.) You have captured the bomb maker from a backyard lab. You are quite sure he has information that will track down the terrorist who has the bomb. You also have a machine that will break his arms and legs one by one.

A. Do you use the machine on the man to help find the bomb?

B. Change the story so that:

  i)   the bus is full of kindergarten children.

ii)   the bus has the American president on it.

iii) the bus has your mother on it.

iv) you are only 80% sure that the bomb maker has any information.

v)   you are only 80% sure that the "bomb maker" is involved at all.

vi) you are only 80% sure there is a bomb at all.

vii) you have other leads, which have an 80% chance of finding the bomber.

Note: a similar question was asked in a BBC world survey of 27,000 people in 2006.

— 59% of people said torture should never be used under any circumstances, even when it would save lives.

— People in Western democracies were more likely to say that it should never be used (e.g. 72% in Britain, 81% in Italy).

— 29% felt that governments could use some torture in certain cases.

ETHICAL THINKERS — ROUSSEAU AND HOBBES

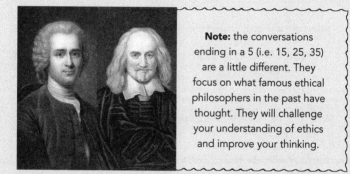

Note: the conversations ending in a 5 (i.e. 15, 25, 35) are a little different. They focus on what famous ethical philosophers in the past have thought. They will challenge your understanding of ethics and improve your thinking.

Jean Jacques Rousseau stated in his earlier writings (he went on to change his mind) that humans were at their best when they lived without society or civilization. People were "noble savages" when they lived in what he called a "state of nature." He thought that it was the act of coming into a society with rules and regulations that made people unhappy and corrupt. It also made them worse people.

Thomas Hobbes thought that a state of nature would be a terrible place where people satisfied their ugly animal instincts without any concern for anyone else. He said it would be a way of life that is certain to prove "solitary, poor, nasty, brutish, and short." Hobbes believed that to avoid this fate, people should band together in a type of "commonwealth" where, people would have to give up some basic freedoms and privileges to a leader in return for protection and some basic rights.

LEFT ALL ON YOUR OWN

Imagine a bizarre thing happening to you at school one morning. At 9:30 A.M., all of the teachers and adults mysteriously disappear into thin air. When students try to leave by the school gates, they bounce back. They can SEE outside, but cannot get there. All the mobile phones go dead, all internet connections are cut: there is no contact at all between your school and the rest of the world.

Even more mysteriously, between 12:00 and 12:01 P.M., enough food appears at the school to feed everyone. There is also a note saying that enough food will appear each day at the same time.

Nothing else happens.

A. What do you think would happen at your school:

   i)   after a day?

   ii) after a week?

   iii) after six months?

B. In particular ask yourself:

   i)   How much do you think people would share and how much would they take for themselves?

   ii) Would leaders emerge? Who would they be? What would they be like?

   iii) Would violence break out?

   iv) Would things get better or worse over the months?

v)   What would you do? What sort of person would you be?

vi) Do you agree more with Rousseau or Hobbes? Do you think that societies "brutalize" us or "civilize" us?

CONVERSATION
36

TORTURE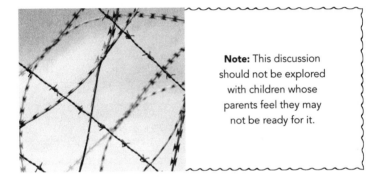
CONTINUED

Note: This discussion should not be explored with children whose parents feel they may not be ready for it.

Imagine that in the example from Conversation 34, you successfully used torture to thwart the bomber. Imagine too that you have used similar torture a number of times to prevent other attacks.

A. Has it become more acceptable to imprison and torture people who are drug traffickers with information about who their suppliers are?

B. Is it okay for other states to imprison and torture you to find out information?

C. Has America become a "repressive" government for using torture as a way of investigating terrorism? Should America's leaders be prosecuted?

D. Do you believe that "no torture" is a moral absolute (i.e. it can NEVER be justified) or something else?

E. Is significant torture worse than murder?

F. Various philosophers have come up with a variety of arguments against torture. They are listed below. What do you think of them? Do you agree or disagree with them?

It is ineffective—some people will lie to stop being tortured.
It is ineffective—hardened terrorists will withstand torture.
Other methods are more effective.
It is against the United Nations Declaration of Human Rights.
Once a country starts torturing people, it won't know where to stop, and people will eventually be tortured for minor or political offences.
Any country that does it is immediately a morally bankrupt state.
You cannot claim the moral high ground against terrorists if you are torturing them.
Any state that tortures people creates a fanatical (and perhaps justified) opposition.
Torture "radicalizes" the actual people being tortured: once released they will seek revenge.
Public support for any war will go down if the troops use torture during that war.
Torture gives the "enemy" a propaganda tool for new recruits.
Torture violates the human dignity of the victim: it dehumanizes them.
Torture destroys the humanity of the torturer: they become more brutal as people.

DONATING TO
EARTHQUAKE RELIEF

Imagine that Puerto Rico has suffered a terrible earthquake. Many thousands are dead and injured and whole towns have been wiped off the map.

A. Would it be good for individual Americans to donate money to Puerto Rico?

B. If the answer to this is "yes:"

    i) Should Americans feel morally obliged to donate money to Puerto Rico?

    ii) Should Americans be legally obliged to donate money to Puerto Rico?

iii) Are Americans legally obliged to donate money to Puerto Rico?

C. If it would be good for Americans to donate money:

i) Should you donate $10 you had no particular use for?

ii) Should you donate your lunch money?

iii) Should you donate your birthday money?

iv) Should you donate money you would have used to buy an iPhone?

v) Should you donate all the money your family had planned to use to go on a holiday?

vi) Should you sell up your house, donate the money, and live in rental accommodation?

D. Answer these questions again, but this time assume that all of the aid money would be "effectively" be used to rebuild schools and hospitals.

E. If you have committed to give $50 to Puerto Rico:

i) Should you instead donate instead to another country where children die every day from causes such as malnutrition or poor health?

ii) Should you only donate to charities in America until everyone has reached a certain standard of living?

iii) Should you donate instead to cancer research?

38

PREJUDICE

A. Through a bizarre coincidence, ten students from the country of Inner Mordavia enroll in your grade. None of them know each other, though they all hum the Inner Mordvian National Anthem to themselves, and pack a strange type of pickled fish sausage in their lunch packs each day. In addition:

i) two of them become terrible bullies of younger kids in the school;

ii) six of them come in the top ten of the term math test;

iii) all ten of them have particularly large noses;

iv) and they have a religion that believes in reincarnation of souls.

v) five of them have parents who owned 24-hour convenience stores in the area and work incredibly hard to keep them open.

Would you be entitled to draw any generalizations about people who come from Inner Mordavia on the basis of the above information? Or not?

If an eleventh person from Inner Mordavia came to your class and sat in the empty seat next to you, would you be entitled to draw any conclusions about them before you started talking to them? Or not?

B. When deciding if you want to be friends with people should you discriminate or choose on the basis of:

i) their interests (same ones as you)?

ii) their intelligence?

iii) their behavior at school?

iv) whether they are gay or straight?

v) whether they live close to you?

vi) whether they are of your race or a different race?

Why/why not? What is the difference between these ways of choosing?

C. What is prejudice? Is it bad? Why?

D. Why do people become prejudiced?

E. If a person is prejudiced because their parents were prejudiced is it their fault?

F. If a high school student feels that they, their families, and their ancestors have been prejudiced against their whole life, is it okay for them to:

   i)   feel anger?

   ii) dislike the race of people who they think have been doing the prejudice?

   iii) steal from the people who they think have been doing the prejudice?

G. It turns out that Inner Mordavia is a landlocked country full of discrimination. Blond people there have been prejudiced against for centuries. The dark-haired people have dominated them since anyone can remember. The 'blond hairs' have been the servants, the slaves, and the lowest on the social ladders. They have had to sit at the back of buses and were not allowed to swim in public pools with the 'brown hairs.' However, the Government of Inner Mordavia has seen the error of its ways. They start up an 'affirmative action' program with the aim of making 'blond hairs' the same as 'brown hairs' within fifty years.

   In it:

   i)   'blond hairs' can get into college with SAT scores 10% less than brown haired people.

   ii) 'blond hairs' will get jobs over brown-haired people if they are otherwise equal at interviews.

   Is this fair? Why/why not?

CONVERSATION
39

LOOTING AFTER [Ⓜ] DISASTERS

Imagine that you were in an earthquake five days ago and that all of the civil society around you had crumbled. The society will probably get working again in a couple of months, but that is not going to help you right now. You are hungry and thirsty.

A. Is it okay to take things from food shops and eat them? Should you only take "staples" or can you take more luxury items like chocolate?

B. Is it okay to take things from food shops five days after the earthquake and sell them to other people?

C. Is it okay to take food from looters to eat yourself?

D. Is it okay to fight a looter to take food?

E. If you were the owner of a food shop five days after the earthquake, would it be okay for you to shoot people who were trying to loot your store?

F. Is it okay for the police to shoot looters?

G. If you are a shop owner is it okay to barricade up your shop to keep your products safe after an earthquake and not hand them out to people?

H. If you were a shop owner, would it be okay to sell your food at twice the normal price after an earthquake?

ETHICAL POTHOLES
AT DUDGEON HIGH

Note: the conversations ending in a 0 (i.e. 10, 20, 30) are a little different. They focus on HOW to think ethically. They are about developing thinking skills. They will sharpen your mind and improve your cognitive capabilities.

There is a school called Dudgeon High where all the students are unethical brutes. They fall into ethical potholes all the time. They are revolting to know and cause misery and pain to themselves and everyone else.

The publishers at "109 Conversations" went undercover into Dudgeon High. They listened to the children's conversations. They recorded some of them. They returned shocked, but determined to share the unethical behavior with the world.

Over the next few pages you will read a description of 16 ethical potholes that the students at Dudgeon High kept falling into. Read over them. Then read the 16 conversations that were recorded undercover at Dudgeon High. Match each conversation with one of the ethical potholes. The answers are on page 253.

Have fun. And make sure you don't fall into the same potholes in your own life.

POTHOLE 1: Everyone does it

This occurs when a Dudgeon High girl justifies the things she does by saying that everyone around her does them as well. By looking around her and seeing the behavior repeated everywhere, she thinks she does not have to ethically justify her behavior. An example of this is a Dudgeon High student illegally downloading music and thinking it is okay because "everyone does it".

POTHOLE 2: They're too big to notice

This occurs when a Dudgeon High boy thinks it is okay to rip off or steal from another organization because the organization is very large. He feels that usual ethical systems about theft, cheating, and other wrongs only apply selectively. An example of this is a Dudgeon High student illegally downloading music by U2, the biggest band in the world.

POTHOLE 3: If you can't beat them, join them

This happens when a Dudgeon High girl holds out for a (usually short) time against something that is unethical. However, when she sees other people around her all doing it, she thinks she is put *at a disadvantage*. Thus she decides to do the same thing as well. (This is different to "everyone does it"—in this case, the girl starts by not doing an act and then changes her mind.) We heard an example of this in which a Dudgeon High girl wrote French words all the way up her arm before a French test because that's what some of her friends did in the last test.

POTHOLE 4: It's not my fault

Dudgeon High boys think that as long as something wasn't their fault in the first place, they have no responsibility for trying to fix it. Even if an act unfairly advantages them and unfairly disadvantages someone else they will not try to change it. We heard an example of this in which a Dudgeon high boy "came first" in a swimming race when he knew that the timers actually got his lane and the lane next to him mixed up.

POTHOLE 5: It's not the worst thing
This happens when a Dudgeon High girl compares her own bad acts favorably to even worse acts, then decides that her own act wasn't so bad after all. People *should* be comparing their wrong acts to "right" behavior, not "even more wrong" behavior. We heard an example of this in which a Dudgeon High girl who took a blue pen from another girl's locker, claimed that it wasn't so bad because she could have stolen the whole pencil case.

POTHOLE 6: It's not illegal
This occurs when a Dudgeon High boy thinks that as long as there isn't a law against something, then it is okay to do it. However, ethics is wider than law. The law only covers *some* of the things that are ethically bad. We heard an example of this in which a Dudgeon High boy cheated on his girlfriend.

POTHOLE 7: The letter of the law
This occurs when a Dudgeon High girl uses a very technical interpretation of a law or rule to get away with something wrong. What she should be doing instead is looking at what was intended by the rule. She will always be looking for "loopholes" in laws and regulations, and will probably one day come unstuck doing this. We heard an example of this in which a Dudgeon High girl stole something from the cafeteria but was picked up by a teacher before she had actually walked out of the door.

POTHOLE 8: Poor me
Dudgeon High boys think that having a lot of commitments or stress allows them to make ethically bad decisions and not have to be responsible for them. They use it to justify anything from cheating in exams to being abusive to another member of their

football team. We heard an example of this in which a boy swore at a teacher but said that it wasn't his fault because he had been stressed out by all the homework he had been given.

POTHOLE 9: It's what my heart tells me

Dudgeon High girls often decide that if they desire something then they can take it and it must be okay (letting their heart or appetite rule). This justifies their decisions. It also means they don't have to think about how their acts hurt other people. This is different to someone using their "gut" to work out if an issue is right or wrong. We heard an example of this in which a girl went out with five different boys even though she was engaged to be married to the Class President. She says it is what her heart has told her to do, so it is okay.

POTHOLE 10: If I don"t do it, someone else will

This happens when a Dudgeon High boy thinks he should do a wrong thing, because if he doesn't, someone *else* will do the wrong thing and get all the reward for it. This often happens when an employee is ordered to do something wrong by an employer—he thinks that if he doesn't do it, he will get fired and the next employee will just come along and do it anyway. We heard an example in which a Dudgeon High boy was working at a fast food restaurant and selling meat he knew to be bad; he said that if he didn't do it, his employer would just get someone else to do it.

POTHOLE 11: They deserved it

This happens when a Dudgeon High girl decides to do something wrong to a person/institution because she has lost all respect for that person/institution. Thus she decides they can be cheated. We heard of a Dudgeon High girl who stole $50 from her employer every week because she thought her employer underpaid her.

POTHOLE 12: Eye for an eye

A Dudgeon High boy thinks that as soon as someone does something wrong to him, it is okay for him to do the same thing (or perhaps something even worse) back. He thinks that revenge is okay and he has not heard the phrase "two wrongs don't make a right." We heard an example of a Dudgeon High boy who tripped a friend after the friend punched him.

POTHOLE 13: It's too small to count

Boys from Dudgeon High think that an unethical act has to be "big" enough before it is really wrong. Thus they think it's okay to do all sorts of small unethical acts because they don't matter. However, small unethical acts (as well as being wrong themselves) can get people used to committing larger acts. We heard of a Dudgeon High boy who copied and pasted a paragraph from Wikipedia into his assignment saying "who's going to notice something that small."

POTHOLE 14: Cognitive dissonance

This happens when people who Dudgeon High girls admire do the wrong thing (e.g. cheat, lie, bully). The Dudgeon High girls *should* stop admiring the person. What they do instead is start to think that the behavior of that person isn't so bad after all. We heard of an example of a Dudgeon High girl who got her lips enhanced at the age of 14, saying that her three favorite hip hop artists had already done it.

POTHOLE 15: I'm good

This happens when a Dudgeon High boy believes that he is a very ethical and good person. Thus he decides that any act that he does must be a good and ethical act, just because he did it. Indeed, this excuse actually stops people thinking ethically at all. We heard a story about the straight-A student of Dudgeon High who is cheating on his girlfriend. He says that because he is a good person, it must be okay to have two girlfriends at once.

POTHOLE 16: The ends justify the means

Dudgeon High girls use this all the time. It allows them to do all sorts of dishonest and unfair things because they are all for some "greater good." Their actions can be for a charity or to "keep the peace." We heard of a Dudgeon High girl who committed identity theft on Facebook in order to investigate who had stolen her $20.

OVERHEARD CONVERSATIONS FROM DUDGEON HIGH

CONVERSATION 1

Girl: Where did you get that yummy doughnut?

Boy: I stole it from the cafeteria.

Girl: You stole it?

Boy: Yeah, all my friends swipe from the cafeteria. What's the problem?

CONVERSATION 2

Boy: Where did you get those nice shoes?

Girl: I stole them from David Jones.

Boy: You stole them!

Girl: What? Do you think David Jones is going to notice one little pair of sneakers missing?

CONVERSATION 3

Boy 2: Hey, how did you do on that test?

Boy 1: Great. I copied off the guy in front of me.

Boy 2: What, you cheated?

Boy 1: Yeah, well, what was I supposed to do? I wasn't going to cheat. Then I saw George copying off Arthur. I saw James copying off Spiro. I realized that if I didn't copy off the guy in front of me they were all going to get better grades than me.

CONVERSATION 4

Boy: Hey look, I came in fifth in the class.

Girl: But you're terrible at math.

Boy: Yeah, the stupid teacher recorded my mark the wrong way around: 95 instead of 59. Yeehah!

Girl: But you're going to get into the top math class now instead of someone who really deserves it.

Boy: I's not my problem if the teacher was too stupid to even copy down a mark properly.

CONVERSATION 5

Boy 1: I got suspended for flushing Bob's history books down the toilet.

Boy 2: How do you feel about that?

Boy 1: Well, I think it's unfair. I could have flushed ALL his books down the toilet. I mean in the old days people used to get their heads flushed down the toilet, not just their books.

CONVERSATION 6

Girl 1: I promised my boyfriend that we'd go out to dinner on Saturday night.

Girl 2: Haven't you told your best friend you're going to her birthday party on Saturday?

Girl 1: Yeah.

Girl 2: Can you do both of them?

Girl 1: Nope. I'm just going to choose which one I'd rather do on the night, and do that.

Girl 2: That's pretty weak.

Girl 1: What's wrong? There's no law against it.

CONVERSATION 7

Boy 1: I came home drunk out of my mind at 12:05 A.M. on Monday morning. I know the exact time because I looked at my watch.

Boy 2: What did your Dad say?

Boy 1: He didn't suspect anything until Wednesday. He said, "Did you come home drunk on the weekend?" I told him "No" and swore blind that this was true. Well. . . it is true, technically. I didn't come in until 12:05 A.M on Monday.

CONVERSATION 8

Girl 1: I told Juliet that she was fat and stupid.

Girl 2: But Juliet always helps you out with your homework.

Girl 1: Yeah, I know. But I've been studying really hard for my exams and not getting enough sleep and I've just been dropped from the hockey team. She'll understand.

CONVERSATION 9

Boy 1: I've left Charlene to go out with Darlene. That girl is a fox.

Boy 2: But you weren't you going to take Charlene to her formal tomorrow night?

Boy 1: What my heart wants, my body takes.

CONVERSATION 10

Boy 1: Oh no, are those shoes you are wearing from Supersports Clothing Warehouse?

Boy 2: Yep, basketball shoes, top of the range.

Boy 1: They're cheap rip-offs from North Korea.

Boy 2: How do you know?

Boy 1: I work there. I pulled off all the "Made in North Korea" labels myself.

Boy 2: You jerk.

Boy 1: My boss made me do it. He said that if I refused he'd fire me on the spot and just get someone else to do it. I wasn't going to lose my job over it.

CONVERSATION 11

Boy: Have a chip. I took it from Smiths the Grocer.

Girl: Isn't that stealing?

Boy: They deserve it. They charge people double what every other grocer does. My parents waste $50 bucks a week in there. We're getting our little bit back from those jerks.

CONVERSATION 12

Boy 1: Scott soaked me with water from the bubbler. My shirt didn't dry for an hour.

Boy 2: What did you do about it?

Boy 1: I got him back. At the end of that period I got his bag and filled it with water.

CONVERSATION 13

Girl 1: I just grabbed half a bottle of water from an eight grade girl's bag. Gee I was thirsty, and it tasted nice.

Girl 2: Did you know the girl?

Girl 1: Nope. I've seen her in the distance, but that's it.

Girl 2: Why didn't you go to the water fountain?

Girl 1: Too far away. Couldn't be bothered.

Girl 2: That's a bit mean.

Girl 1: No it's not. Water's free. And it was only half a bottle.

CONVERSATION 14

Boy 1: I'm going to cheat on my girlfriend tonight, because that new girl Becky from Slinky High is hot.

Boy 2: You always hated cheating on people. You told me last year how much you thought it sucked.

Boy 1: Yeah, that's what I thought last year. I've changed my mind.

Boy 2: That's pretty rough on your girlfriend.

Boy 1: What's the problem? In the last year Andrew Guernsey from the Bulldogs got caught with a cheerleader while he was engaged to someone else. Plus the golfer Cheetah Hoods, he had 2,352 affairs. Even Senator Todgot was caught having an affair. It's not so bad after all.

CONVERSATION 15

Girl: I've just copied Max's whole iTunes library onto my iTunes. 10,000 songs!

Boy: Didn't you win the "Dudgeon High Award for Ethical Behavior"?

Girl: Yeah, that's why I did it! I'm an ethical person. So I thought, if I think it's okay to do it, then it has to be.

CONVERSATION 16:

Boy 1: Hey, I just gave $20 to a cancer research charity. I am so good.

Boy 2: But you didn't have any money at lunchtime when we were at the cafeteria.

Boy 1: Oh yeah, I mugged a seventh grade boy after school and took his money. It was for a good cause.

SAVING SURVIVORS AND RECONSTRUCTING AFTER AN EARTHQUAKE

After a recent massive earthquake in Haiti, the United Nations (UN) stated that the phases of aid in a devastated earthquake area were to focus on rescue missions first and then shift to providing food and shelter for the survivors. Because UN agencies thought that a significant number of people could still be saved each day after the earthquake, they focused on rescue, not food and provisions. On the sixth day after the Haiti earthquake, 40 people were pulled alive from the rubble. On the tenth day two people were pulled from the rubble. The UN finally shifted to relief on the eleventh day.

A. Imagine that you were the person in the UN making the decisions. How long after an earthquake would you focus on pulling people alive from rubble instead of providing necessities like food and shelter for the survivors? Why this long?

B. Should aid agencies move immediately after an earthquake to providing resources for survivors?

C. If you knew that halting providing food and shelter for hundreds would mean that one child trapped in the rubble could be pulled free, would you do it?

D. Should aid agencies rebuild broken buildings to the *same* standard they were before the earthquake? Or should aid agencies rebuild broken buildings to a *better* standard that they were before the earthquake?

E. The UN claims that there is a high level of corruption in Haiti. Should aid be withdrawn until the government shows that it is serious in stamping out corruption?

F. Should aid agencies give the money to local organizations and contractors to rebuild? Or should they organize the whole thing themselves?

G. Should the military of a country such as the United States or France take over co-ordinating aid efforts after an earthquake?

42

FATE —
ARE PEOPLE MORALLY
RESPONSIBLE?

A. If you are going to fall onto the road in front of a truck tomorrow afternoon, is this already decided?

B. Is it determined that the sun will rise tomorrow?

C. If you are going to get into a fight with your best friend this afternoon, is it determined that it will already happen?

D. If you are going to grow up and become a fraudulent money trader, who rips people off and goes to jail, is this already decided? Why or why not? If it is already "decided," then are you responsible for your actions?

E. Think about terrorists who blow up a plane because they believe that they will get amazing rewards in the afterlife for doing this. Are they morally responsible for their actions? Why/Why not?

The following ideas may help you in your discussion:

- **Hard determinism** says that you are a puppet, controlled by all of the choices and physical acts that have already occurred. This theory relies on the work of Sir Isaac Newton, who stated that the whole world is like a mechanical wind-up clock, with every physical movement governed by the iron laws of physics such as gravity and motion. So, too, every choice a person makes is governed by choices that were made before this time, which in turn are governed by choices made before this time, and so on. We may have a sense of free will, but it is a complete illusion.

- **Libertarianism** says that there is no real cause and effect. Every decision and action is based on choices made at that moment. Ethical decisions are based on each person's character acting on a particular situation at a particular time. No matter how difficult the situation (e.g. poverty, drugs, crime) some people will always "rise above" it to make good choices.

- **Soft determinism** is a halfway point between hard determinism and libertarianism.

  - On the one hand it says that the choices we make are based on a whole variety of elements such as previous choices, values, environment, etc. The combination of all these different things is so complicated that the result is almost random.

  - On the other hand, freedom to act is real and completely voluntary. You make choices from moment to moment all the time.

FREE WILL AND
LIFE FACTORS

Imagine twins, cruelly separated at birth due to a mistake at the hospital.

- **James** got terrific genes (including intelligence and good looks), a stable, loving and wealthy family, great schooling, lots of extra opportunities, such as lessons and travel, and a great set of friends.

- **Luca** got terrible genes (including low concentration and terrible looks), a dysfunctional, abusive and poverty-stricken family, bad schooling, no additional opportunities, and some very poor role models for friends.

A. What is the likelihood of James and Luca being "successful" in life? Will Luca be able to rise above his start in life?

B. Below are some factors that sociologists suggest affect peoples "free" will. Which ones do you think are the most and least important?

i) their family situation

ii) the genetic pool they come from

iii) their socioeconomic status and environment (money, school, privilege, etc.)

iv) the peer group that they fall into

C. Is the government responsible for trying to give Luca more opportunities? Does Luca deserve help from the government?

IS THE OLD MAN EVIL?

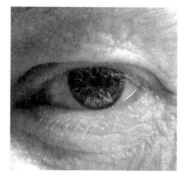

An old man rides into a small village with a cart behind him. The cart is boxed up and nobody can see inside it. He stops at the village square and a crowd gathers around him. He waves a gold staff above his head and begins to speak.

"Ladies and gentlemen," he says, "I have the offer of a lifetime for you. For absolutely no cost I will drain away everybody's sadness and pain with my golden staff. Everybody in the village will be completely happy and content for the rest of their lives. All you have to do is mind my cart."

"What's in the cart?" asks one person.

"It doesn't matter," says the man. "You can put the cart in your dungeon, or in your furthest field. I promise you on my life that nothing will ever come out of it and nothing from it will ever affect you. You can completely ignore it for the rest of your lives.

I don't care."

The people in the square are very excited at this and go to get the mayor of the town. The old man repeats his offer to her. The mayor has a meeting with the town elders, and they decide to accept the offer.

"Done!" says the old man, and points his staff at them. Immediately the people can feel their worries, pain, and sadness draining away from them. They are all overjoyed.

The mayor declares a public holiday and there is much eating and drinking among all the happy people. Then one woman goes over to the cart and peeks inside.

She almost faints at what she sees. Inside is a poor, wretched, miserable girl, aged about ten. She is filthy and starving and writhing in pain on the floor.

The woman runs over to the other villagers and they try to get the girl out of the cart, but they cannot. They turn and challenge the old man.

"What is that girl doing in there?" the mayor shouts. "How could you do this to her?"

"I have done nothing wrong," says the old man. "When I drained all of your pain and sadness and misery away with my golden staff, I had to put it somewhere. So I simply put it all into the girl."

"That is completely evil," says the mayor in horror.

"It is not," says the man, "There is *exactly* the same amount of pain in this society as there was before. It's just that it is now in a different place. I have not caused any pain at all. I have only moved it from one place to another."

Has the old man done anything wrong?

> **Remember:** if you come up with one answer, try playing "devil's advocate" to see what the opposite point of view would be.

119

CONVERSATION

45

ETHICAL THINKER — ^M
IMMANUEL KANT

> **Note:** the conversations ending in a 5 (i.e. 15, 25, 35) are a
> little different. They focus on what famous ethical philosophers in
> the past have thought. They will challenge your understanding
> of ethics and improve your thinking.

Immanuel Kant stated that if a person wanted to act ethically, then he/she had to look at whether the act was *right* or not in itself (not make a judgement on the basis of its consequences). This is known as a "deontological" approach. So Kant would say "don't lie" because it's wrong even if lying might lead to good consequences (e.g. lying to your grandmother about how much you liked an ugly sweater she knitted you). Kant said that if you are trying to work out whether something is right or wrong, you should ask yourself "What would things be like if everyone did it?" This is called the categorical imperative.

A. Can a moral law really be universal? Are the following ethical statements universal?

    i)   Do not kill.

    ii)   Tell the truth.

    iii) Do not stick a needle into a person's eye.

B. Kant stated that to check if an act is ethical, you should ask what the world would look like if everyone did the same act. What would the world look like if everyone did the following acts?

i)   illegally downloaded music

ii) lied to their grandmothers about how much they like her ugly knitted sweaters

iii) punched someone who pushed them in the hall

iv) cheated on their girlfriends/boyfriends

C. The following cases might give Kant some trouble.

i)   You are downstairs at home and your father is upstairs. The Mafia turn up with bazookas and ask you where your father is.

   — What would Kant tell you to do?
   — What would you do?

ii) You are a surgeon and you have just been told that your whole family has been killed in a car accident by a drunk driver. A moment later the drunk driver is wheeled into the hospital needing care. You are the only surgeon there.

   — What would Kant tell you to do?
   — What would you do?

iii) Exactly at the moment he is about to discover the cure for cancer, Dr. John Noble goes into sudden heart and lung failure and is rushed to hospital. As it turns out the murderer Skug Skunkley is also in hospital. He has a terminal illness and his organs are completely compatible with Dr. Noble. You are a surgeon who could transfer the organs.

   — What would Kant tell you to do?
   — What would you do?

FRIENDSHIP
(PART ONE)

A. Who are your best friends? What makes them your best friends?

B. If someone *really* wants to be your friend, but you don't like them very much, do you have to play with them at least sometimes?

C. If your best friend loves playing chess and you hate it, are you obliged to play some chess, just to make her happy?

D. Should you be friends with your friend's friends?

E. If your friend's friends are mean to you, and your friend does not defend you, is he really a friend?

F. Can someone have too many friends? Can someone have so many friends that he/she doesn't have any *real* friends?

G. Would best friends ever tell on each other? What if your best friend stole a $2000 ring from a shop and planned to sell it?

(See Conversation 100: Friendship (Part Two))

KILLING PEOPLE
ON A RAILWAY LINE

A. You are in a signal office that is on a bridge over a railway line. You see a runaway train (without anyone in it) hurtling under the bridge. You look with horror over to the other side of the bridge. On the same track there are five railway workers, all about to be killed. You don't have time to call out to them and they wouldn't hear you anyway. However, you can throw a switch to change the direction! You look down the alternative track and there is a 17-year-old boy quietly listening to his iPod on the other track. Do you throw the switch?

B. Change the scenario so that instead of a boy listening to the iPod on the second track, there are four more workers. Do you throw the switch to kill the four workers, or do you leave the switch as it is and kill the five workers?

C. You are in the signal box on the bridge. Sitting on the side of the bridge is a 17-year-old boy quietly listening to his iPod. You have time to jump in front of the train. Do you push the boy off the bridge and possibly get killed?

D. You are a doctor in a hospital. Five railway workers are suddenly brought in to the emergency room because a runaway train has struck them. Miraculously, they are not already dead. However, each needs a different organ transplant (lungs, liver, heart, kidney, and gall bladder) to survive. Sitting in the waiting room is a 17-year-old boy listening to an iPod. His blood and organ types are compatible with all the maintenance men. Do you kill him and harvest his organs for the five workers?

> **Note:** this dilemma is known as the "railway dilemma" and is one of the most famous in psychology.

ACCEPTING DIFFERENCES

A. What would the *whole world* be like if everyone had the same opinions and abilities as you? What would be fun about it and what would be the problems?

B. Would you prefer it if the world was full of copies of you?

C. List all of the differences below from MOST different (1) to LEAST different (14).

    i)   preferring strawberry ice cream vs. preferring chocolate ice cream

    ii) doing homework at night vs. mugging strangers at night

    iii) moderate Christians vs. moderate Muslims

iv) fundamentalist Christians vs. fundamentalist Muslims

v) outgoing vs. shy

vi) liking basketball vs. liking football

vii) liking basketball vs. liking chess

viii) good at basketball vs. not very good at basketball

ix) good at English vs. not very good at English

x) people born in 1998 vs. people born in 1938

xi) interested in other people vs. not interested in other people

xii) using violence to solve your problems vs. using discussion to solve your problems

xiii) liking the Democrats vs. liking the Republicans

xiv) believing everyone should co-operate vs. believing everyone should lie and cheat their way to the top

D. What TYPE of differences seemed to matter the most?

E. What TYPE of differences seemed to matter the least?

F. Imagine spending a lot of time with someone who is very different to you. What are the good and bad things that would come of it?

G. Should people who are different to you try to persuade you that their difference is better than yours? If so, when?

H. What things do you believe that you would want to convince other people about? What things WOULDN'T you want to convince other people about?

WHAT IS BULLYING?

A. Do you think that the following incidents are bullying? Are they wrong? Why?

i) Ben insults Vince's mother every day for a week.

ii) Ben and Vince have previously played on the same soccer team. Vince has now left the team to join rowing. Ben insults Vince's playing skills, his social skills, and calls him a "quitter."

iii) Vince tries hard in class. Ben makes jokes about Vince in class, and twice has ripped up Ben's homework.

iv) Vince insults Ben's mother. Ben punches Vince.

v) Ben calls Vince "dogbreath" once as they walk down a hall.

vi) Ben calls Vince "dogbreath" every day for a week.

vii) Ben calls Vince "dogbreath" every day for three days, writes it on his backpack, and tells all of Vincent's friends that he has dogbreath.

viii) Ben calls everyone "dogbreath" as he walks down the hall.

ix) Vince is a Native American. Ben calls him "red man" in the hall.

x) Vince is Finnish. Ben calls him "white finny" in the hall.

GENERALIZATIONS

> **Note:** the conversations ending in a 0 (i.e. 10, 20, 30) are a little different. They focus on HOW to think ethically. They are about developing thinking skills. They will sharpen your mind and improve your cognitive capabilities.

Do you think there is anything wrong with the following statements?

- Americans are good at sports.

- Tall people are better at basketball.

- Asian people have black hair.

- Dogs are friendly.

The above statements may be true a lot of the time, but they are not true all of the time. This means that they are generalizations. You can spot a generalization by putting ALL in front of the sentence. If the sentence is still true with ALL in front of it, then it is probably true (e.g. ALL candy is bad for your teeth). If it looks shaky with ALL in front of it, it may be a generalization that you wouldn't want to rely on too much because you might get bitten (e.g. ALL dogs are friendly).

Why does this matter? Sometimes generalizations lead to prejudice against a group, which is what can make them ethically dodgy.

A. What prejudice could some of the following sentences lead to?

   i)   Overweight people are lazy.

   ii) People who vote Republican are selfish people who are in it for themselves.

   iii) People who vote Democrat are lazy people who don't want to work hard.

   iv) Refugees want to jump to the front of the line to get into America to make money.

   v)   Refugees are poor innocent victims fleeing torture and death in their own country.

Often the solution to all this is simply to put a word like "some" "many" "a few" in front of the sentence (in fact this sentence starts with just such a word. . . "often"). This can drain the sentence of a lot of its prejudice and allow us to talk about individuals more ethically. These words are (usually) called qualifiers.

B. Try making up some generalizations and then put one of the following in front or within the phrase. How much better have they become? If you can't think of any of your own, try some of the ones below.

   •   A few

   •   Can be

   •   A significant number

   •   Often

   •   Usually

i)   All students at Bareknuckle High are good at football.

ii)   All swans are white.

iii)   Computer games cause students to be unmotivated.

iv)   Sports are dangerous.

v)   Climbing Mt. Everest is dangerous.

vi)   Smoking results in lung cancer.

BULLYING
CONTINUED

A. If a group of 13-year-olds crashed onto a beautiful desert island where there was enough food for everyone and plenty of swimming and fun to be had, do you think there would be any bullying? Why?

B. If there were no adults around your school would there be more bullying or less? Why?

C. Imagine a school where nobody ever bullied anyone. What would it be like?

D. Why is it that people bully?

E. Are bullies victims? When?

F. Why do you think people bully other people?

G. What can you do to make sure you do not become someone who bullies?

H. What is the difference between "joking around" and bullying?

WHAT SHOULD BE DONE TO BULLIES?

A. What should a school do to students who:

i) bully for the first time?

ii) bully someone over a long period of time?

iii) bully a number of people even though adults have tried to help him/her and punished him/her before?

B. What should a victim do when he/she is being bullied? Why might these things be hard to do?

C. What should a parent do if their child tells them they are being bullied at school? Should they contact the school?

D. What should bystanders or friends of the victim do when they see someone being bullied?

53

MAKE UP YOUR OWN SCHOOL RULES

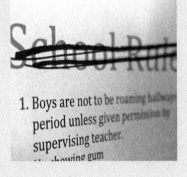

You and your family have been made the Principals of "Happysunny High." Unfortunately Happysunny High is neither happy nor sunny. It is a wild place where bad students rule the playground, good students cower in fear, and good teachers cower in even greater fear. The major issues are:

- bullying of other students

- theft

- terrible behavior in the classrooms

- damage to property

When you look to see the school rules, you find that there aren't any. "No wonder the place is such a mess" you say to yourself. You decide to make up a new set of school rules to deal with the issues. How to *enforce* these rules will be hard, but that will be a job for later. Right now, your main job is to make up a set of rules for a school so that everyone can learn, feel safe, and be respected.

A. What are some of the rules that you make up for Happysunny High?

B. What do you do to people who break those rules?

WHAT IS CYBERBULLYING?

A. Which of the following incidents do you think is cyberbullying? Which three are the worst?

i) Belinda texts or gets on Facebook for three nights in a row and tells Verity that she is a big fat loser and nobody likes her.

ii) Belinda texts Verity once to say she is a big fat loser and no one likes her.

iii) Belinda and Brittany say nasty things about Verity on Facebook, thinking that they are in a private chat room. It turns out that the room is public. Stella reads what Belinda and Brittany have said and passes it on to Verity.

iv) Verity is nauseous and throws up in class. Belinda takes a photo of it and posts it on Facebook.

v) Verity holds a birthday party on Saturday night. Belinda doesn't like Verity. She posts an invitation for a rival party saying "Belinda's party! More food than Verity's! More boys than Verity's! More fun than Verity's!" Everyone goes to Belinda's party, and Verity is left to have a birthday party with one friend, her parents, her dog, and some limp streamers.

vi) Verity has a very embarrassing accident at camp. During the holidays, Belinda texts four friends saying "Guess what! Verity pooped her pants at camp." The four friends pass it on to four friends and so on.

B. You and cyberbullying:

i) What should you do if you are being cyberbullied? Who should you tell? What do your parents expect?

ii) What should you do if you know someone who is being cyberbullied?

iii) What should you do to make sure you never accidentally BECOME a cyberbully?

55

ETHICAL THINKER—
JEREMY BENTHAM

Note: the conversations ending in a 5 (i.e. 15, 25, 35) are a little different. They focus on what famous ethical philosophers in the past have thought. They will challenge your understanding of ethics and improve your thinking.

Jeremy Bentham said that "nature has placed mankind under the governance of two sovereign masters, pain and pleasure." He held that people should try to maximize the amount of *pleasure* in the world. (He also asked that his skeleton be dressed and kept on display after his death—and it was.)

He came up with the idea of Utilitarianism. This is a principle that says an act is good (or not) depending on how much pleasure or happiness it gives all people. If it gives more pleasure than pain it is a good act. If it gives more pain than pleasure, then it is a bad act.

In other words you are judging acts by their consequences.

A. Have a look at the following conversations in this book and see what a utilitarian like Bentham would have done. Would you agree?

    i) The pain remover (Conversation 44)

    ii) The railway dilemma (Conversation 47)

B. Do you think the following acts are fair? What would Bentham think?

    i) Your five-year old cousin makes you a terrible birthday card with your name spelt wrong and a picture on it that looks like a collapsed tepee. He asks you if you think it is nice. You say "Yes."

    ii) You steal five cents out of every person's bank account in America and send it to famine relief in Africa.

WHY CYBERBULLYING IS BAD

A. What is different about cyberbullying and face-to-face bullying?

B. How is writing something about someone different from saying it?

C. How is sending a text about someone different from saying it?

D. How is texting someone at home different from abusing someone at school?

E. How is texting someone at night different from texting during the day?

WHY CYBERBULLYING IS BAD

The Youth Advisory Council has given six reasons why they think cyberbullying is so bad. Which do you think are the best reasons and why? *(Note: They are all good reasons.)*

- **Repeat** — The fact that the insults, comments or footage can be preserved either by the person who was bullied or others means that the target may read or view them repeatedly, re-inflicting harm with each reading or viewing.

- **Remember words** — Those young people who are bullied in person will most likely not remember every word that was said, but those bullied online are able to repeatedly read or view the damaging material.

- **Audience size** — The size of the audience that is able to view or access the damaging material increases the humiliation experienced by the target, which is likely to increase the damaging impact of the event.

- **Know bully** — Many young people are friends with or know their cyberbully, either through school or other personal connections, increasing the potential for embarrassment and humiliation.

- **Campaigns** — Social networking sites such as Facebook allow cyberbullies to engage in campaigns against particular persons that may involve many others.

- **Speed** — The speed at which harmful messages can reach large audiences also plays a major part in making cyberbullying so damaging to the targets.

CAPITAL PUNISHMENT
(THE DEATH PENALTY)

The killer Blade McCaverty has just been caught!! The evidence is quite overwhelming. He is a serial gangster and random killer. In a ten-year spree of mayhem and murder he has shot half a dozen people in organized crime raids and randomly shot another half a dozen people from his car window while they were walking down the street.

There is a public outcry that the death penalty should be re-introduced. Before the trial, the American government establishes an "investigative committee" to consider the arguments for and against the death penalty.

On this committee will be two judges, two criminal lawyers, two academics, a prison guard, an ex-prisoner, two members of the adult public, and you.

You need to go into the committee fully briefed to work with these other senior people. The law you recommend will apply to Blade McCaverty and other future serious criminals.

A. Do you think Blade McCaverty should be executed?

B. How do the following ideas help your thinking? Which ones do you agree with most?

- **Retribution** — When something terrible is done, it is proper for the society to take revenge (or vengeance) in proportion—"An eye for an eye."

- **Imprisonment** — Life in prison without chance of release could be "worse" for an offender than execution.

- **Deterrence** — People are less likely to do something bad if they know that there is a terrible price to pay for it.

- **Brutalizing** — A whole society may become more harsh when the people in it know that the law includes a death penalty.

- **Mercy** — A civilized, compassionate society needs to show that it is humane.

- **Hypocrisy** — You cannot show that something is bad by doing the same thing yourself.

- **Mistakes** — Even law courts can make mistakes.

MAKING PROMISES

A. If you promise to go to a friend's party, but then have to go to a family wedding that night, have you broken your promise?

B. If you promise to give a friend your homework to copy, but then decide this is a bad thing to do, have you broken your promise? Is it fair?

C. If you promise a friend to go to their party, but then a party from a more popular person at school comes up, should you break your promise and go to the second party? Why/why not?

D. What is a promise? Why do people make them? How important is it to keep them?

E. What would your family/school/society be like if no one kept their promises?

F. Should people never promise anything in the first place, just to make sure that they never break their promises?

G. Imagine that you are kidnapped and forced to promise to give all of your savings to the kidnappers in order to be released. Then you manage to escape. Have you really made a promise to the kidnappers?

59

MEDICAL ETHICS AND  THE GOVERNMENT

A. Imagine that you are a doctor working with the military. You are co-opted into a "secret anti-terrorism" unit. It turns out that the unit is hurting Al Qaeda members from Afghanistan who they strongly suspect have information about future terrorist attacks in New York. They want you to make sure that the Al Qaeda members do not get too sick or hurt. Do you:

i)   Resign (which may involve "deserting")?

ii) Resign and go to the media?

iii) Refuse to co-operate with this unit?

iv) Work to give the prisoners aid to lessen their pain?

v) Work to keep the prisoner "fit enough" to be hurt further?

B. You are a doctor in the prison system and must carry out the death penalty by means of lethal injection. You do not agree with capital punishment. Do you:

i) Prepare the prisoner for the lethal injection?

ii) Administer the lethal injection?

iii) Be involved in a system in which three needles are inserted into the prisoner and three serums are injected by three different doctors? Two of the serums are harmless, while the third is fatal. Neither you nor anyone else will ever know which of the three doctors administered the fatal serum.

iv) Resign?

CONVERSATION 60

BEING CONSISTENT

Note: the conversations ending in a 0 (i.e. 10, 20, 30) are a little different. They focus on HOW to think ethically. They are about developing thinking skills. They will sharpen your mind and improve your cognitive capabilities.

Brief explanation: If you are using a couple of different arguments to make an ethical point, then they have to be consistent with each other in order to stack up. That means that the different justifications should all be true at the same time. If not all the justifications can be true at the same time, then you need to get rid of one of the arguments.

Do you think the following arguments are consistent?

A. We should rob that bank.

    i)   The bank is huge and they won't miss the money.

    ii)   Banks are uncaring and it doesn't matter if they miss the money.

iii) Capitalism is bad and robbing banks will help bring banks down.

B. We should free all the animals from the local pet store.

i) Keeping animals in cages is cruel.

ii) Animals should be allowed to roam free.

iii) We shouldn't care about the feelings of pet shop owners who keep pets.

OTHER ARGUMENTS

C. I really respect Jane Smith as Secretary of State.

D. I met Jane Smith at a dinner party and boy was she boring.

E. I really respect your views.

F. If you don't like my haircut, I am not going to respect your views any more.

G. I think the world is going downhill: people are selfish, the climate is out of control, and there will probably be a nuclear war.

H. I love waking up every morning and starting the day.

61

MEDICAL ETHICS— TESTING DRUGS ON PRISONERS

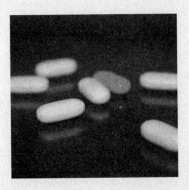

You are a doctor involved in medical research. A new strain of the flu virus appears in cats in Indonesia. It is much more deadly than "bird flu." You have heard stories about the virus transferring to humans. This virus has the potential to devastate populations if it moves into cities and through other countries. You are working on a vaccine. However, your research would be much more effective if you had humans to experiment on and, in particular, give the virus to. You could work on animals, but it is much less effective.

The Prison Warden brings to your (secure) laboratory ten murderers. She says the government has rushed a secret law through Congress that allows you to experiment on these prisoners in any way you like. This includes infecting them with the virus. Do you do it?

62

MEDICAL ETHICS AND KIDNEY TRANSPLANTS

Imagine you are a kidney surgeon. You have the following two patients on your books who will die if they do not get a transplant:

- **Joe** is a ten-year-old boy who loves football, his mom, school, and going surfing.

- **Maria** is a 40-year old nurse. She has an eight-year-old son and a six-year-old daughter who she loves like crazy. Two kidneys come into your surgery.

You find out:

A. They were stolen from an impoverished Indian homeless person who is dying in a Delhi hospital.

OR

B. They were stolen from a poor subsistence farmer in Northern India who died.

OR

C. They were stolen by medical thieves from an American backpacker in India who is now on life support in a Delhi hospital.

OR

D. Two poor Indian farmers sold one kidney each for $50 (people can live with one kidney).

OR

E. Two poor Indian farmers sold one kidney each for $5000. This is enough money to last them for several years.

Do you transplant them?

Your school's principal has decided that teachers will get jobs on the basis of interviews with an interview panel made up of the Principal, the Deputy Principal, and a student. The student they have picked is you! She tells you that she values your ideas because as a student you have to sit in the classes each day.

She explains to you that "discrimination" is about making distinctions and that the panel has to choose between potential teachers. For example, she says, the panel may choose to discriminate on the basis of whether a teacher has ten years' experience or none. However, you quickly become worried about some of the things the Deputy Principal is using to discriminate. Some of them seem unfair.

Which of the following statements do you think are unfair ways of choosing who should be the teacher? Which ones are fair?

A. That Mrs. Patel, she's Indian. I don't like Indians.

B. That Mr. Jones, he's American. We've got enough Americans, we need more variety.

C. That Mr. Lee, he's too short. I've got nothing against Chinese people, but a teacher should be able to reach to the top of the whiteboard. Don't hire him.

D. That Mr. Khan, he has studied at the University for ten years and knows twice as much as all the other teachers. Let's hire him.

E. That Mr. Jallop, he's been a teacher for 45 years. He's too old now. Don't hire him.

F. That Mrs. Frindle, she's pregnant. She'll be off work again in six months. Don't hire her.

G. That Mr. Black, he's got such a high voice none of the children will do what he says. Don't hire him.

H. That Mr. Green, he's so good looking all the girls will fall in love with him. Don't hire him.

I. That Mrs. Nesbitt came in wearing what looked like a sack, hadn't ironed her clothes, and her hair was all over the place. Don't hire her.

J. That Mr. Smith is gay. Don't hire him.

CONVERSATION

64

THE GOOD LIFE PIE

Imagine that you get to split some of the things that go into making a good life as pieces of a pie. You get to choose how big each piece is by drawing it onto the pie. How big do you make each piece? Pieces to include:

A. A happy family, including parents and children

B. A lot of money to buy things like a big house, great car, clothes, and all the gadgets you want

C. A lot of good friends

D. A lot of education, learning, and wisdom

E. Travelling around the world to see all sorts of amazing things

F. An interesting and worthwhile job

G. Parties, parties, parties

H. A chance to help other people—either in your job or by volunteering

CONVERSATION

65

ETHICAL THINKER—
JOHN STUART MILL

Note: the conversations ending in a 5 (i.e. 15, 25, 35) are a little different. They focus on what famous ethical philosophers in the past have thought. They will challenge your understanding of ethics and improve your thinking.

John Stuart Mill was a utilitarian like Bentham (Conversation 55). However, unlike Bentham, he said that you should aim for *happiness* not pleasure. Happiness for him included cultural and spiritual elements, while he saw pleasure as only for lower beings. He wrote that "it is better to be a human dissatisfied that a pig satisfied."

A. Would you rather be a pig that was always satisfied or a person who was usually dissatisfied?

B. As a human, would you give away your intelligence if it guaranteed that you would be satisfied for the rest of your life?

C. Would changing the following rules increase pleasure for the greatest number? Would they increase happiness?

i) Voluntary school attendance

ii) Equal money for everyone

iii) Compulsory family relationship classes

iv) Wii in every house

Bentham was an *act* utilitarian. This is because he thought you needed to judge each individual *act* based on how much happiness it caused. By contrast, Mill was more of a *rule* utilitarian. This meant you had to makes up *rules* to promote the maximum happiness for the maximum number of people.

D. (Same question as Conversation 45) Exactly at the moment he is about to discover the cure for cancer, Dr. John Noble goes into sudden heart and lung failure and is rushed to the hospital. As it turns out the murderer Skug Skunkley is also in the hospital. He has a terminal illness and his organs are completely compatible with Dr. Noble. You are a surgeon who could transfer the organs.

i) Would an act utilitarian like Bentham do it?

ii) Would a rule utilitarian like Mill do it?

iii) Would Kant (from Conversation 45) do it?

iv) Would you do it?

DUTY

A. Do you think you have the following *duties* or not? Why?

i) A duty to help someone up who trips over on the street next to you.

ii) A duty to protect someone who is being punched and kicked by robbers in the street.

iii) A duty to give all of your pocket money away to desperately poor people in India.

iv) A duty to listen to people who have called your home phone asking you to buy something.

v) A duty to give money to the person next to you in the cafeteria line who cannot afford chocolate milk.

vi) A duty to visit your old and sick grandmother.

vii) A duty to help with some chores around the house.

viii) A duty to do as many chores around the house as your parents.

ix) A duty not to use a lot of electricity because it contributes to climate change.

x) A duty to do your homework.

xi) A duty to help your younger brother/sister with homework he/she can't do.

B. What is a duty? Who do you have duties to? For what? Who has duties to you?

THE CURE FOR AIDS

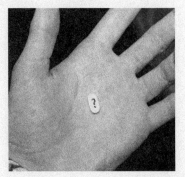

Your company has developed a cure for AIDS. It cost you five billion dollars. You market it in the developed world for $4000. Most of the AIDS victims in the world live in Africa, where $4000 is totally out of reach of most of the population.

A. Do you market a "generic" version of your drug for sale in Africa for $50? This will risk the generic drug being imported back to the developing world.

B. Do you give the drug away in Africa?

C. Do you keep selling the drug for $4000?

CONVERSATION 68

S E X

For work experience, you are sent to intern at the teenage gardening magazine *Growing New Fruits*. Surprisingly, among the articles about soil composition and optimum fertilizers, they have started up a 'moral sex therapy' column authored by Professor Ficus. More surprisingly, they ask you to fill in for Professor Ficus when he gets sick. Letters are flooding in and you have to write answers to the following questions. How do you answer the following?

A. Dear Professor Ficus,
My boyfriend and I have been going out for two months. I just want to kiss on the couch. My boyfriend wants to go further. I tell him 'no,' but it makes him really moody and liable to listen to Metallica really loud. He says he won't leave me because he loves me, but I am still worried. Should I let him go further?

Chloe (age14)

B. Dear Professor Ficus,

My girlfriend Katie only lets me hold hands and kiss her. Everything else is off limits. I like her, I guess, but there are plenty of other girls out there who would let me go a lot further. In fact, two have posted letters into my locker over the last week saying what they would like to do to me. Should I drop Katie and hitch up with someone else who will let me go all the way?

Tony (age 16)

C. Dear Professor Ficus,

I asked my parents about what to do to make sure you didn't have babies. They threw saucepans at my head and said that was none of my business until I was eighteen. It's okay—I found out everything I needed to know from the internet. But should they have talked to me about it, even if they didn't want to?

Steve (age 13)

D. Dear Professor Ficus,

I would like to get it on all the time with everyone I meet of the opposite sex. At every party, after school, and after games. I don't care what the person is like. I just want to have fun and they just want to have fun, and what's the harm in that? My friends are rude to me about it. What do you think?

Chris (I am not going to tell you if I am a guy or a girl) (age 16)

E. Dear Professor Ficus,

I think you should only go all the way if you love the other person and plan to marry them. Physical love is the glue that holds true love together and I don't want to cheapen it. However, I am worried that I am missing out. What do you think?

Scott (age 15)

RELATIONSHIPS,  SOCIAL STANDING, AND BODY IMAGE

A. Ruby is going out with John, who is a good guy with pretty average looks. She meets Creighton who is a good guy with amazing looks. Creighton is interested in her. Should she dump John and go out with Creighton?

B. Ruby is going out with Fred who is a good guy with average popularity. She meets Fabio who is a good guy who is massively popular and gets invited to heaps of parties. Fabio is interested in her. Should she dump Fred and go out with Fabio?

C. Felicia has perfectly okay looks, average weight, and very small lips. She is going out with Johnnie who says 'I love my woman to be hot.' She is worried that he may leave her for someone who is better looking. Should she:

i) go on a diet?

ii) go to gym five times a week?

iii) wax?

iv) scour magazines for how she can look good and then spend forty-five minutes each morning in front of the mirror getting ready?

v) get plastic surgery to make her lips fuller?

D. Rob likes Adora, but Adora is out of his league and only goes out with hot guys. If Rob works outs six days a week, bulks up with the protein powders, and stops taking his little brother to the park, he can have a ripped body in six months. If Adora isn't around, he'll probably be able to hook up with someone else. Should he do it?

E. Marcia is a freshman at Vapid Heights High School. She gets hold of the mugshots of all of the freshmen guys at the school and creates a program where all her girlfriends (and anyone else) can rate each guy from 1-5. This then creates a 'Top 40.' She says that she will not publicly rank the last twenty guys in the year. Is this morally wrong?

F. If we spent ten years hearing about how moles were sexy and all of the magazines were full of women with moles on their faces (with hair coming out of them) and all of the most famous actors went out with ladies who had at least two moles, would moles end up being sexy?

G. If we spent ten years hearing that 'personality was all that mattered' and magazines stopped writing about how people looked, and all the most famous actors went out with people with interesting personalities, what would happen? Would looks stop mattering? Why/why not?

H. Is our society too interested in body image? Or not?

I. If society is too interested in body image, should we go along with it anyway?

J. When thinking about getting together with someone, what things should matter most to you? Rank what matters most to you.

  i)   looks

  ii) personality

  iii) sense of humor

  iv) intelligence

  v)   chemistry

  vi) body

  vii) willing to get with me

  viii) kind/good/thoughtful

  ix) popular

  x)   willing to get physical

  xi) interested in the same things as me

TWELVE LOUSY ARGUMENTS

Background: When people want you to believe something no matter what, they often put together lousy arguments to help their case. However, these are not hard to spot. There are 12 of them listed here along with some things that you can do with them as a family.

A. Write them down, stick them up around the television, and then watch the news. See how many arguments get used.

B. Write them down, stick them around the television, and then watch some ads. See how many arguments get used.

C. Try spotting the argument after each of the explanations.

D. One person reads out the fake speech (see end of this conversation) made at a girls' school about why boys shouldn't be let in. Each paragraph contains a different lousy argument. See if you can spot them.

Note: you may want to do them all at once,

or just do one or two at a time.

LOUSY ARGUMENT 1: To the Person

Sometimes, when people are trying to disprove an argument, they ignore the argument altogether and instead attack the person who made the argument. In other words, they attack the person not the argument itself. This is cheating. An example of this would be "Mr. Storey tried to make me do my math homework, but he smells."

Which of the following two arguments is an example of "to the person?"

A. Dr. Jones says that eating Weet-bix™ in the morning keeps you healthy, but everyone knows that he is a drunk.

B. Ian Thorpe, swimming superstar, says "Eat Weet-bix™!" But everyone knows Weet-bix™ aren't enough to make you a superstar.

LOUSY ARGUMENT 2: Unfalsifiability

For an argument to be any good, you should be able to disprove it. For example, if my argument is "gravity on earth makes books fall to the floor," then this could be *disproven* by letting go of a book and watching it float away. If an argument cannot be disproven at all, then it is not much of an argument in the first place. This is because it is unfalsifiable. An example of an unfalsifiable argument is "All around us is a world of invisible little green goblins. When you lose things it is actually the little green goblins taking them. When you find things, it is the goblins putting them back. We cannot detect these goblins with either our senses or our scientific instruments."

Which of the following two arguments is an example of "unfalsifiability?"

A. That madman Saddam Gaddafi is so clever that he can hide nuclear bombs in his country without anyone noticing. If we can't find them, that just shows how clever he is at hiding them.

B. That madman Bill Bush hides nuclear weapons and this shows what a dangerous madman he is.

LOUSY ARGUMENT 3: Argument from Authority

This argument asks you trust someone without them giving you any reasons why. It simply asks you to believe in their authority. This argument is used a lot in advertising. Most of the time when a star tells you to buy something, he/she is simply exercising argument from authority (by contrast an expert or an experienced person *could* give you advice). An example of this is "Don't question the president because she is the president of the country."

Which of the following two arguments is a better example of "argument from authority?"

A. The American Olympic swim team says, "Use Valvoline® Motor Oil in your car."

B. Nine out of ten dentists say, "Use toothpaste because it reduces tooth decay."

LOUSY ARGUMENT 4: It Happened After, So It Was Caused By

Sometimes people will claim that if an event happened at one time (e.g. Jane came to school in September) and another event happened later (thefts started in October), then the later event was *caused* by the earlier event. This would lead you to think that Jane was a thief. However, the two events may not actually be connected. Even if they are connected, one probably did not *cause* the other. An example of this is, "Ever since women got the vote, politicians have worried more about their image and the

Amazonian rainforests have been threatened with destruction." Which of the following two arguments is an example of "It happened after so it was caused by?"

A. I walked under a ladder. One minute later a bird pooped on my head. Walking under ladders brings bad luck.

B. I robbed a bank. I got caught. You shouldn't rob banks.

LOUSY ARGUMENT 5: Non Sequitur

This happens when one point does not relate to the other. Usually the conclusion is not related to the argument or evidence. The term "non sequitur" comes from the Latin "it does not follow." For example, your father could tell you that you should be a soccer player, because he was a great soccer player when he was young. However, how good a soccer player he was has nothing to do with how good you will be. This makes the statement a non sequitur.

Which of the following two arguments is an example of "non sequitur?"

A. Fifty per cent of people who smoke die of smoking related diseases. Do not smoke.

B. I don't like the label on the new Coke can. Lemonade is better to drink.

LOUSY ARGUMENT 6: Straw Man

This happens when someone uses the most extreme example of an argument in order to prove (or discredit) the *whole* argument. "Football players are stupid, look at Bob Jones" is an example of a straw man argument. Bob Jones may be the most stupid man in football, but that doesn't tell us anything about the intelligence of the thousands of other people who play the game.

Which of the following two arguments is an example of "straw man?"

A. Don't buy anything off the internet. I know someone who tried to buy a book, and their whole identity was stolen. They lost all of their money and their house.

B. Be careful of your privacy settings on Facebook otherwise a lot of people can look at your pictures.

LOUSY ARGUMENT 7: Unfair Extension

This happens when someone takes an argument to extremes. It is similar to the straw man argument but different in that the focus is on the argument itself rather than offering extreme examples to illustrate the point. An example of an unfair extension argument would be the following exchange between a student and teacher:

Student: "Could we please have a little less homework?"

Teacher: "Fine, if that's how you feel, let's cut all homework. In fact, if you don't want to learn, why don't we just cut school out altogether?"

The teacher's response extends the student's argument into places the student never intended. This extension is unjustified and unfair. Which of the following two arguments is an example of "unfair extension?"

A. Jack: "I think that people did some things better in the past."

Sarah: "Fine. Why don't you just go back and live in a cave?"

B. Judy: "I like sushi."

Felicity: "Yuk. How can you like the idea of raw fish?"

LOUSY ARGUMENT 8: Begging the Question

This is the hardest of the lousy arguments. Begging the question happens when you actually *assume* that an argument is correct, even as you argue for it. For example, we might say that a law about school funding is a good law just because it has been passed by Congress and is already in place. In doing this you have *assumed* that the law is good just because it is a law. It is an argument that goes around and around in circles.

Which of the following two arguments is an example of "begging the question?"

A. We should make John the class president because he is the best person for the job.

B. The president should be able to do what he wants because he is the president.

LOUSY ARGUMENT 9: Weasel Words

Weasel words are used when someone wants to excuse an action or statement by merely changing the terms for it. For example Lucy may claim that Jane didn't invite her to a party. Jane may respond that it wasn't a party, saying it was just a gathering of people who came around to her house. Changing the term "party" to "gathering" doesn't explain why Lucy was not invited.

Which of the following two arguments is an example of "weasel words?"

A. I haven't lost my homework, it's just long-term misplaced.

B. John: "Have you been talking in class?"
Jane: "No, but I was whispering."

LOUSY ARGUMENT 10: False Analogy

False analogy occurs when you make a wrong comparison, often using what's called "metaphors" or "similes." For example, a parent could say "Raising children is just like teaching lions to do tricks. You have to whip them into shape." Perhaps you do have to whip lions to make them do tricks, but this doesn't mean you have to whip *children* to teach them. The comparison, or analogy, is false.

Which of the following two arguments is an example of "false analogy"?

A. Looking at the water is like looking at a shimmering blue curtain.

B. Doing homework is like baking a cake. Sit there for an hour and it's all done.

LOUSY ARGUMENT 11: Appeal to Pity/Emotion

Emotion as part of an argument can work. However, when it is used to make *all* of an argument, it means that the argument is in trouble. For example, if a father said to a teacher, "If you could see the miserable face of my little Nazim at 7:30 P.M., you wouldn't assign any homework ever again," he is simply appealing to emotion. If the father instead said Nazim was miserable because he had already done three hours of homework and was about to do three hours more, then there would be, perhaps, a good argument. However, if Nazim is miserable just because he doesn't like doing any homework at all, it's not much of an argument. Then it is simply an appeal to pity.

Which of the following two arguments is an example of "appeal to emotion?"

A. If you could see how happy children are eating ice cream, you would give it to them for breakfast, lunch, and dinner.

B. No, don't do it… please.

LOUSY ARGUMENT 12: The excluded middle

This occurs when someone insists you take an extreme point of view with them. If you don't adopt *their* extreme position, they assume you have taken the opposite extreme. This leaves out all of the many positions in the middle. An example of this is: "Either you love your country or you hate it." In fact, there are a thousand positions between love and hate; "liking" your country, being "fond" of your country, feeling "neutral" about your country. In saying "if you don't love it, you hate it" you make almost everyone who may have a criticism to make about the country sound like they hate it.

Which of the following two arguments is an example of "the excluded middle?"

A. Yeah, that's right, take Joshua's side. He's always right, I'm always wrong.

B. Why don't you ever listen to me? Are you ignoring me?

TRANSCRIPT OF SPEECH MADE BY EUNICE P. TIRADE TO THE PANKHURST SCHOOL FOR GIRLS

Well, good morning to you, fine upstanding young ladies, one and all of you. I have heard that you are thinking of opening the gates of your school to boys as well as girls.

Don't do it, girls, don't do it. I have many good, sound, and solid reasons for this. For a start I knew a boy once. Jimbob was his name. Oh, angel-faced little thing he was, butter wouldn't melt inhis mouth. Yet he went on to burn his whole school down. Now, is that the sort of person you want wandering around the halls of Pankhurst School for Girls?

Secondly, having boys at Pankhurst School for Girls would be an insult to all of the previous Headmistresses of Pankhurst School: Headmistress Jones, Headmistress Smith, Headmistress Fununculus. None of them had boys at the school. They obviously didn't believe in boys. Are you going to say that all of these great women were wrong? That they were foolish, doddering old simpletons? Are you going to disrespect their memories and their legacies by spitting in their eyes and trampling on their academic capes?

Of course there shouldn't be boys here. Go and have a look at the Pankhurst School for Girls Charter. The rules of the school say: "A school for girls." It's there in black and white. I want to tear my hair out when I hear people saying "Bring in boys." Can't they read a simple document in English.

I know of a school in Florida that admitted boys, after a proud tradition of having only girls for 100 years. And do you know what happened the next day? The whole place was blown away by a typhoon. Children clinging to palm trees all up and down the coast. Do you want this for Pankhurst? Our beautiful classrooms and ovals ripped to shreds and carried out to sea, just so that boys can sit next to girls in a geography class? Oh, it makes my blood boil to even think that someone could wish such devastation and destruction on their own school.

Now I hear on the Pankhurst School for Girls grapevine that all of this nonsense was started by none other than Mrs. Jones in the English Department. Well, really. I mean, is she not the ugliest woman ever born? She should be digging a hole for herself to crawl into, rather than strutting around the school with that tuber of a nose and those pig like little eyes. Furthermore with her little, spider-like frame and fetid breath, no boy would want to go within 20 feet of her, haw, haw, haw. So, don't listen to Mrs. Jones!!!

I tell you, having boys at Pankhurst is just like dropping a firecracker into your good old hearty vegetable soup. I did that once when I was a nurse in the last war. SPLAT it went. Oh, what a sight to see, a multicolored rainbow of farm fresh produce arching through the air. All over the field hospital it was. Is this what you want for Pankhurst: mess, muck, and mayhem? You're going to have to be the ones to clean it all up.

I have just come from the Old People's Home where old Edna O'Grady lives. She's a Pankhurst Old Girl but now she's blind, deaf, and suffering from advanced leprosy. Oh, how her remaining eye would spill over and weep if she heard that Pankhurst was going to have boys. Her heart would break and there would be nothing left but a body, ravaged by the years' and reduced to jelly by the cutting cruelty of a school that no longer cares. Are you willing to do this to a woman who worked her fingers to the bone for her country?

Plus, if you are thinking about educating boys next year, what are you going to let in the year after: unemployed adults looking to be re-educated, the population of Africa? Why stop there? Let's throw the door right open. What about all the farmyard animals who would like an education? Once you start this, who knows where it will stop? Before long daughters of Old Girls will be sharing their classroom with a Xhosa warrior and a Friesian cow.

I'll tell you another reason why this is madness—boys are just boys! It's in their nature. That's all there is to it, no getting around it, no avoiding it. And what you are not even starting to consider is the strange morphic electric field all around Pankhurst School for Girls that makes our girls three times more intelligent that girls at other schools. This strange energy force is maintained by a small army of electric gremlins that can only be seen by me, Eunice P. Tirade. If boys come to Pankhurst, I can assure you that the morphic field will collapse and disintegrate. You will only have yourselves to blame when your girls become dull-witted and boorish.

Furthermore, there are some people saying that maybe we should at least discuss the issue more, have more contract with boys schools, that sort of thing. Don't listen to them! They just want to fill the place. There will be boys hanging off the rafters all over the place. These people are the enemy. If you are not with me on this, you are against me, and I will hunt you down and have you expelled. Expelled I say!! Expelled with a whip!! Expelled with slavering hounds baying at your feet!!!

I know I have convinced you with my superior reasoning and profound thinking. Thank you, thank you. I must go to my next appointment now. Your Headmistress has ordered me a taxi. Thank you, thank you.

(Pause)

Ahh, no Headmistress, that's not a taxi, it's an ambulance. What are you thinking? And hold on, that's not my coat. It's white. And the arms are tied behind its back. What are you doing? Headmistress? Headmistress? Aghh!!! Help! Help me! Just remember girls. . . NO BOYS!!!

(Siren)

PARENTS, CHILDREN, AND RULES

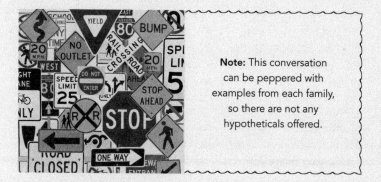

Note: This conversation can be peppered with examples from each family, so there are not any hypotheticals offered.

A. Why do parents get to tell you what to do?

B. Are there times when you should do what parents tell you to without questioning? Why?

C. Are there times when you *should* question what parents tell you?

D. What makes a good set of rules by parents?

E. Would you prefer clear rules at home, or rules that change from day to day? Why?

F. Can parents be wrong?

G. Can parents be right, even if you think they are wrong? How could you tell?

H. Should you get to bargain and negotiate with your parents, or should the rules just stand?

I. Should parents punish you? How and why?

J. Should parents ever hit you?

K. Is shouting at you like hitting you, or is shouting something else?

L. When do you get to know as much as your parents?

M. Should you even have this type of conversation with your parents, or does it "undermine their authority?"

DECLARING WAR  ON CANADA

In an unlikely set of events, imagine that you are elected president of the United States of America. You employ your family as your closest advisors. However, the global landscape has changed and Canada has become a seriously dangerous neighbor. Canada has:

- built up its conventional military so that it rivals yours.

- declared that the U.S. is a "nation that should be destroyed."

- converted to a new religion and held demonstrations outside mosques, synagogues, and churches.

- has banned U.S. products from its shops.

Would you declare war on Canada if:

A. Canada has invaded the U.S.?

B. Canada has invaded Wyoming only and established a military camp?

C. Canada is making lightning raids through the Northern U.S., terrorizing the residents, stealing products, and then retreating?

D. Canada has invaded Eastern Russia for its oil reserves?

E. Canada has flown two planes into the Empire State Building and the Trump Tower?

F. Canada has announced that it has chemical and biological weapons of mass destruction and is planning to use them on you?

G. Canada has revealed that it has a nuclear treatment plant that will be able to produce weapons grade material within 12 months.

H. Canada has assassinated your Vice President (a.k.a. your mom).

I. Canada has created an economic blockade around America that prevents ships coming into the U.S.?

J. Canada had created powerful trading blocks with half of the countries in the world. It will only deal with these countries on the condition that they boycott U.S. trade?

K. Canada shuts down all schools for men and makes them wear top-to-toe jerseys with only a slit at eye level. Men cannot be employed and they are shot with tasers by the police if they are seen in public without their wives?

L. Canada ruthlessly suppresses all internal dissent with long imprisonment terms and the routine use of torture?

M. Canada rounds up all Europeans and Africans within their borders and begins to massacre them?

ACTING ETHICALLY IN ^M THE MIDDLE OF A WAR

You have declared war against Canada. Do you then engage in any of the following acts? *(Remember, this is an ethical discussion, not a video game.)*

A. Use a biological weapon that will devastate all of the military barracks in Toronto and halt military planning in its tracks.

B. Firebomb the entire city of Toronto with conventional weapons.

C. Torture prisoners that you capture for information.

Ethicists have had a variety of views about what an ethical act is in the middle of a war *("jus in bello")*. Some are described below. What do you and your family think about them?

A. There is no such thing as a just war, so there is no point discussing just and unjust acts within it.

B. If you have declared a just war, it is your responsibility to get it over with as quickly as possible, and this can include extreme measures (such as firebombing a city).

C. If the cause is "right" (e.g. defeating an evil regime) then a country is entitled to act in any way in a war.

D. Unless a country acts decently in a war then they are no better than their enemy. People are still expected to be ethical in war.

CONVERSATION 74

WHO ARE WE RESPONSIBLE TO FOR CLIMATE CHANGE?

Note: This discussion follows statements made by the overwhelming majority of climate scientists that the earth is warming partly due to human activity. It also has as its starting point the information that there is a high probability of temperature rises of at least 2 degrees by 2100, with various predictable and unpredictable results.

As both individuals and communities, when making decisions using resources, do we have an ethical obligation to:

A. future generations who are not yet born?

B. individuals in the developing/Third World who are more vulnerable to the effects of climate change?

C. animal species that may face extinction?

D. the biosphere/planet as a self-regulating system that has developed over billions of years?

ETHICAL THINKER —
ELIZABETH ANSCOMBE
(AND ARISTOTLE)

> **Note:** the conversations ending in a 5 (i.e. 15, 25, 35) are a little different. They focus on what famous ethical philosophers in the past have thought. They will challenge your understanding of ethics and improve your thinking.

Elizabeth Anscombe looked at all the ethical philosophers from Conversations 35, 45, 55 and 65 and thought they were on the wrong track. She thought that the best way to think about ethics was to think about "virtues," what kind of person we could be and what type of life we should live. Doing all this correctly would lead to happiness. She went back to Aristotle's writings and his thoughts about character (see Conversation 15). The sorts of virtues that Anscombe and other philosophers thought were admirable included elements such as compassion, benevolence, patience, and kindness. One of the ways of working out what is ethical is to look at people who you admire ethically and ask what features they inspire in you.

A. Who are some of the people who you most admire? Why?

B. Who are the best people you know or know of—the people you think are the most ethical? Why do you think this?

C. What sort of person do you want to be when you are 35? What do you want to be remembered for after you die?

D. What are two of the best things about you now? What are two of the worst things about you now?

E. Have a look at the very long list of virtues below. What are some of the virtues that you have a lot of, and which ones do you not know so much of?

F. Choose two virtues you think you don't have a lot of. What could you do to get more of them?

G. Is it possible to have all of these virtues?

Acceptance	Fortitude	Peacefulness
Appreciation	Friendliness	Perceptiveness
Assertiveness	Generosity	Perseverance
Awe	Gentleness	Purposefulness
Benevolence	Grace	Reliability
Caring	Gratitude	Resilience
Charity	Helpfulness	Respect
Cheerfulness	Honesty	Responsibility
Commitment	Honor	Righteousness
Compassion	Hope	Self-sacrifice
Confidence	Humanity	Self-discipline
Consideration	Humility	Serenity
Contentment	Humor	Service
Co-operation	Idealism	Simplicity
Courage	Independence	Sincerity
Courtesy	Initiative	Steadfastness
Creativity	Integrity	Strength
Curiosity	Joyfulness	Tact
Determination	Justice	Thankfulness
Devotion	Kindness	Thoughtfulness
Dignity	Love	Tolerance
Diligence	Loyalty	Trust
Empathy	Mercy	Trustworthiness
Enthusiasm	Mindfulness	Truthfulness
Fairness	Moderation	Understanding
Faith	Modesty	Wisdom
Fidelity	Openness	Wonder
Flexibility	Optimism	
Forgiveness	Patience	

76

WHAT TO DO ABOUT
CLIMATE CHANGE?

Note: This discussion follows statements made by the overwhelming majority of climate scientists that the earth is warming partly due to human activity. It also has as its starting point the information that there is a high probability of temperature rises of at least 2 degrees by 2100, with various predictable and unpredictable results.

A. There are many things that as individuals we could *choose* to do about climate change. However, are there things that we are ethically obliged to do? Have a look at some of the ideas below. Which ideas are most like your own point of view? Why do you believe this?

i) We do not have to do anything—the only solutions come from the government.

ii) We do not have to do anything that may reduce economic activity, our standard of living, and the standard of living of the other people in our country.

iii) America does not have to do anything until China make the same commitments.

iv) We should make non-difficult adjustments to the way we live—convert to green power, turn off lights, drive energy-efficient vehicles.

v) We should vote for parties that are committed to reducing the levels of carbon in the atmosphere to levels recommended by scientific experts.

vi) We should to make large-scale adjustments to the way we live such as selling cars, relying on public transport, moving to smaller houses, only eating minimal meat, among others.

vii) We should downsize our consumption to such a level that if every person on the planet had our standard of living, the carbon levels would still be sustainable.

B. Various solutions have been suggested using technology that does not work now. Much research is being done on these various solutions. Is it ethical to rely on technological solutions that may exist in the future? Why/why not?

CONVERSATION

77

CHANGING LANES ON THE ROAD

A. You are in the right lane of a two-lane road. The right lane is full of slow moving cars. You know that the left lane is going to end in 300 feet. It is almost empty. Should you:

i) stay in the right lane?

ii) drive ahead in the left lane and then merge back in?

B. You are in the right lane of a two-lane road. The right lane is full of slow moving cars. The left lane is moving much more quickly, but you know that there are often parked cars in this lane, which forces drivers to merge back right. Do you:

i) stay in the right lane?

ii) drive ahead in the left lane and merge back into the right lane when you encounter a parked car?

C. Is there any such thing as pushing in and cutting lines on roads? Are the rules on the road different to the rules in the lines at the cafeteria, for example?

78

JUSTICE AT THE CAFETERIA

A. You have been waiting in the line at the cafeteria. People are behind you. A friend comes up and asks you to buy them a hamburger.

   i) Has your friend "cut" in the line? Do you buy him a hamburger?

   ii) Would it make any difference if there were only one hamburger left and you knew that the person behind you wanted a hamburger too?

B. You have been waiting in line at the cafeteria. People are behind you. Ten of your friends come up and ask you to buy them hamburgers. They give you enough money to do this. Do you buy them?

C. You are waiting in line in the cafeteria. A senior boy pushes in front of you. You say "Hey, you are cutting the line." He tells you that when he was younger, people always pushed in on him, so now it is his turn to go to the front of the line. Is this okay? Why/why not?

D. You are in line at the cafeteria waiting to buy a hamburger. The person in front of you just got $100 for her birthday. She has decided to spend it on hamburgers for all her friends and clears out the cafeteria. Thus, there are no hamburgers left for you. Has she done something unfair? Have you been treated unfairly?

E. The cafeteria is at the side of the school. The class nearest to it has a teacher who always lets them out right on time. As a result they are always at the front of the line and always get the best things from the cafeteria. Is this fair? Should the teacher hold them back?

F. Have unfair things happened in the cafeteria line at your school? What are they? What should have happened?

79

HOW TO TREAT YOUR BROTHERS AND SISTERS

A. If you were given a movie pass for two people, are you more likely to take your brother/sister or your best friend? Why?

B. If the world ended, there was one can of soup left, and you could only share it with one person, would you be more likely to share it with your brother/sister or your best friend? Why? Is there a difference between this and a movie pass?

C. Should your parents share things equally between your siblings and you, or should it depend on how well you perform (e.g. how hard you work, how well you do at school, how well you behave)?

D. Your little sibling messes up your room looking for a toy. Should you mess up his/her room so that he/she knows how bad it feels? Why?

E. You love pizza and hate Chinese food. Your sibling loves Chinese food and hates pizza. Your parents refuse to make two dinners at once. What should happen at the dinner table?

F. Your sister/brother brings home a friend who you think is horrible and bad for your sister/brother. What should you do?

   i) Be horrible to the friend and hope to break up the friendship.

   ii) Tell your sister/brother that you don't like the friend.

   iii) Do nothing, it's not your business.

   iv) Tell your parents all about the awful new friend.

   v) Do something else.

G. Would you rather have a brother/sister who was just like you, or one that was completely different? Why?

H. Are you obliged to share things in the house with your brother/sister (e.g. the last two cookies in the box)? Or is it "everyone for themselves?"

I. What are the best things about your sibling? Do they know you think this? Should you tell them, or keep it to yourself?

CONVERSATION

80

BEING COMPREHENSIVE

Brief explanation: Being comprehensive means taking everything into account when you make a decision. It requires that you *stop* when you think you are about to make a decision, and check that you have not left anything out.

Some things you could think about when trying to be comprehensive include:

A. Do you have all of the facts?

B. What are you trying to achieve?

C. What would be the *consequences* of your decision?

Imagine that you are your school's principal. Becky is brought to you by a teacher because she has stolen another girl's iPod from her bag during gym. Becky and the other girl hardly know each other. Becky's own iPod broke last week. You have the power to expel Becky from the school.

You have to decide whether to expel Becky or not. Do you do it? What are all of the questions you should ask yourself when making your decision? You can make up additional facts about the case if it helps you think about your decision.

ROAD ETHICS:
LETTING PEOPLE IN

A. You are in the congested right lane of a two-lane road. Someone has driven up the much emptier left lane and there is now a parked car in their way. Do you let them merge into your lane?

B. You are on a congested main road. Someone is waiting to turn left into the main road from a side street. You know that the side street allows people behind you on the main road to drive up and re-enter at the same place as you. Do you let them in?

C. You are in the left lane of a road in slow moving traffic. Someone has travelled very fast up the right lane, which is a "right turn only" lane. They want to be let back in front of you to continue going straight ahead. Do you let them in?

CONVERSATION
82

S P E E D   L I M I T S
O N   T H E   R O A D

A. Imagine you are the head of the Department of Transportation. You have been told by the president to make up new speed limits. What do you think the speed limit should be on the following roads?

i) a main road

ii) a side road

What extra information would you like to make a more informed decision? Why might this be a question about ethics? Whose rights are you weighing up when you make your decision?

B. Are people ethically obliged to obey the speed limits on American roads? If they don't are they being unethical?

C. If your mother goes at 62 mph in a 60 mph zone, is she breaking the speed limit? Is she being unethical?

D. On an average straight suburban road with houses on both sides, at 5:00 P.M, is it ethical to drive at any of the following speeds?

i) 50 mph	v) 65 mph	ix) 80 mph
ii) 51 mph	vi) 69 mph	x) 100 mph
iii) 60 mph	vii) 70 mph	xi) 190 mph
iv) 61 mph	viii) 75 mph	

E. Answer the question above again with the knowledge that the speed limit on that road at 5:00 P.M. is 70 mph.

Does your answer change if you have:

i)   passengers in the car?

ii) a baby in the car?

iii) a children's soccer game going on in a park on one side of the road?

F. The right hand side of a two- or three-lane road is often for people who wish to overtake (or go faster). You are in a 60 mph zone. People often travel in this zone at 70 mph. Is it ethical to drive in the right hand lane at 62 mph?

DRUGS

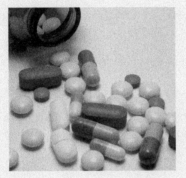

Imagine that a new chocolate-soma pill was distributed for free at your school by the Government. If you chew it, the whole world looks like friendly, happy paradise. Everywhere you see fields and rivers of gold. Buildings are palaces made from rare, edible rubies and diamonds. Everyone is delighted and laughing all the time. Everything is fascinating—every blade of grass and every molecule of dust. And the feeling goes for hours. There is no way you can sensibly communicate with other people or do any work, but you don't care. When the pill wears off there are no side effects. When you go home you find that your parents have been given whole packets of pills too, and you can go back to friendly happy paradise whenever you want. It turns out everyone has got a limitless stock of these pills.

A. What would happen to your school after a day?

B. What would happen to your school after a month?

C. What would happen to the country after a week?

D. What would happen to the country after a year?

E. Would people be able to stop, or would the pills become addictive?

F. What is the difference between:

i) taking a pill, and

ii) feeling happiness because you did well on an assignment or scored the winning goal in a game?

G. Is the happiness you feel taking the pill real? Why?

H. What would happen if everyone at the school used a drug such as marijuana regularly?

I. What happens to individuals who use drugs such as marijuana regularly?

J. What is addiction? How does it start? How does anyone become addicted?

K. Should people be prevented from taking the first step towards an addiction? Or is it up to them?

L. Some states have decriminalized marijuana use for medical reasons. Should they?

HEALTH, DRUGS, AND  YOUNG PEOPLE

A variety of studies have demonstrated conclusively that marijuana, alcohol, and other drugs can have a very bad effect on the developing brain of a teenager. They can lead to depression, loss of memory, aggression, schizophrenia, and other conditions.

Secondly, similar studies have shown that young people's brains are still developing—this means that their judgments may not be the same as adults. As the National Institute of Drug Abuse writes; 'One of the brain areas still maturing during adolescence is the prefrontal cortex—the part of the brain that enables us to assess situations, make sound decisions, and keep our emotions and desires under control. The fact that this critical part of an adolescent's brain is still a work-in-progress puts them at increased *risk for poor decisions (such as trying drugs or continued abuse). Also, introducing drugs while the brain is still developing may have profound and long-lasting consequences.'*

QUESTIONS

A. Should an adolescent be allowed to make decisions that harm his/her own health? Is it his/her choice?

B. At what age, generally, do you think that a young person can make a mature decision about the risks involved in:

   i) crossing the road?

   ii) riding their bike to school?

   iii) smoking pot (in a state where this was decriminalized)?

C. To what extent should a teenager be allowed to make their own mistakes and learn from them?

D. When thinking about doing something dangerous, does a teenager have a responsibility to think about his/her parents and the time they spent raising him/her? Or is it his/her own life?

E. Is an adult entitled to 'ban' something that is dangerous to a teenager's health?

F. What should happen when adolescents break rules that are designed to protect his/her health? Anything?

G. Why is taking drugs criminal in most states?

H. Should it be illegal for teenagers to smoke marijuana?

I. Should a teenager obey the state's laws about marijuana even if she does not agree with them? Why?

ETHICAL THINKER —
JOHN RAWLS AND THE
MIND GAME

John Rawls believed that each person had an equal right to as
much liberty (freedom) as they could have, as long as their liberty
allowed other people to have just as much freedom. Thus, our
freedom to travel where we like is consistent with everyone else's
freedom to travel where they like. By contrast, we do not have
a right to the freedom to bash other people because this would
interfere with other people's right to be safe as they walk down
the street.

As a way of getting people to think about justice and freedom,
John Rawls made up "the mind game." Using the scenario below
you can do it with your family right now.

THE MIND GAME

You and the rest of your family are present at the creation of the world. From the blackness of space you can see (in fast forward) the continents forming and reforming, the mountains rising and falling, the land expanding and cooling.

A large curtain is then placed between your family and the rest of the world. This veil is known as the "Veil of Ignorance." Each of you then discovers that you are going to live in one of the societies that will form on the world. However, you will not be told what your position in that society will be.

You could be anybody. You could be the ruler, you could be the richest person in society, or you could be a genius (or all of these). On the other hand, you could be the poorest, most underprivileged person, starving in the street. You could have a physical deformity, you could be extremely sick, or have no intelligence. You could have had parents who have encouraged in you the values of hard work, or you could have had parents who have encouraged in you the opposite values.

You just don't know.

You need to choose and make up the set of laws for the society that you are going to live in. Almost every law will advantage some people and disadvantage others. You may *try* to act in your own "self interest," but this will be difficult, as you don't know who you are going to be.

Would you include the following laws?

i) Everybody should be paid the same amount of money for working the same number of hours.

ii) Students should have the right to leave their parents at the age of 14 and go to live in special "youth camps," run by adults, with people their own age.

iii) There should only be government schools, no private ones.

iv) Taxation should only be used to fund the police force; everything else should be paid for by people themselves.

v) People who steal property, without being violent, should not be sent to jail; instead they should be rehabilitated in intensive training camps.

vi) People who steal property, with violence, should be executed.

vii) At the end of your life all of your property is returned to the state.

viii) If a person is charged with murder, and the judge is 80% sure the person is guilty, the person should be convicted and punished.

ix) Everybody between the ages of 18–60 who is healthy must either be in full-time education, full-time childcare, or employment.

A TEENAGER'S CAR

A. When someone first gets their licence, is it ethical for them to drive any of the following cars?

   i) a tiny two-cylinder car with almost no safety features

   ii) an average four- or six-cylinder car

   iii) a large SUV

   iv) a Hummer

   Explain your answer.

B. When someone first gets their licence (at the age of 17, 40, or 70) is it ethical for them to drive in any of the following situations?

i) faster than 50 mph

ii) with three passengers

iii) with music playing very loudly

iv) with a hands-free device that allows them to talk on their mobile phone

v) with any alcohol in their bloodstream

Why/ why not?

C. Cars can kill people—drivers and pedestrians.

i) Should only "top of the line" cars with every safety feature be allowed on the roads?

ii) Should the speed limit everywhere be 30 mph?

iii) Should people have to do a "safe driving course" every 12 months?

iv) Should we force people to use public transport unless there is no alternative?

v) Should we replace cars with horses and carts?

87

WHEN IS A "NEW  LIFE" A HUMAN?

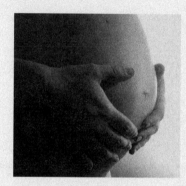

A. When is a "new" set of genetic material a human life?

i) When it is a one-cell organism in a woman

ii) When it is a one-cell organism in a test tube

iii) When it is an "embryo" in a woman

iv) When it is an "embryo" in a test tube

v) When it is 8 weeks old (lungs just started, heart beating)

vi) When it is 14 weeks old (hair, skin, muscles, bones, liver)

vii) When it is 25 weeks old (eyes, fingerprints, eyelashes)

viii) When it is born

ix) When it can recognize others (several weeks after birth)

x) When it can survive "by itself" (two years of age)

B. At what fetus age can a mother ethically decide to terminate a pregnancy?

C. Whose decision should it be whether a mother terminates a pregnancy: the mother, the father, the doctor, or the state?

D. On what basis could a mother terminate a pregnancy?

i) The fetus is going to be a baby with a lot of physical and/or mental disabilities.

ii) The fetus is a boy and the parents want a girl.

iii) The mother does not want to have a child at all.

E. Bob and Jane have an only child, Patsy. Patsy has a rare blood disorder and will die without a bone marrow transplant. There is a 50% chance that any brother or sister will have matching bone marrow with Patsy (there is almost no chance anyone else will). Jane falls pregnant with a new child. Tests show that this new child will not have matching bone marrow for Patsy. Jane and Bob want to terminate this pregnancy and try again for a sibling that will have matching bone marrow for Patsy. Is this ethical?

ONLINE ETIQUETTE AND AGE RESTRICTIONS

A. People are not supposed to go onto Facebook until they are 13 years of age. What do you think of this? Should the age restriction be higher or lower?

B. Should parents be the friends of their children on Facebook? Why/why not?

C. Should people have to use social networking sites such as Facebook in public areas of the house? Or can they use them in private areas such as their bedrooms?

D. Should parents be able to stop their children from social networking? Why/why not?

E. Do the same rules of "manners" apply online as in the real world? If not, how are they different? Should they be similar?

F. Should boyfriends/girlfriends be able to break up online, or should they always do it face-to-face? Should you end a friendship online?

G. Can you be "friends" with someone online who you have never met? Why/why not?

HOUSEWORK

A. How much housework is it fair for each member of the family to do? Why?

B. Should parents do more housework than children? Why?

C. Should children not have to do any housework at all? Why?

D. Should housework be linked to an allowance, or should these be separate?

E. If you have a busy life (sport teams, homework, music lessons, etc.) should you be expected to do less housework?

F. Which of the following would you consider to be reasonable housework? Which is not?

i) washing the dishes/stacking the dishwasher

ii) cooking for your parents and their friends

iii) fixing the roof

iv) cleaning your room

v) grocery shopping

What is the difference between reasonable and unreasonable housework?

G. If your older sister kicks up such a stink about housework that she ends up doing very little, is it fair for you to do much more than her?

H. Should you get to choose which housework you do?

I. What is the best way to divide up housework among the family?

J. Is it fairer to divide up housework on the basis of time (e.g. "we're all going to spend half an hour cleaning") or jobs (e.g. "I'll cook the dinner and you can stack the dishwasher")?

K. If you don't get any housework, should you ask for some?

L. Imagine your parents said to you, "We want you to do two hours extra of math every week. In return, we will let you off doing any housework." Would you take the offer? Why/why not?

M. Is housework for children slavery? Is housework for parents slavery?

N. If your parents had servants to do all the housework, do you think you would grow up any differently?

CONVERSATION
90
UNIVERSALIZING

Note: the conversations ending in a 0 (i.e. 10, 20, 30) are a little different. They focus on HOW to think ethically. They are about developing thinking skills. They will sharpen your mind and improve your cognitive capabilities.

Brief explanation: When you universalize you ask what would happen if everyone else did the same thing that you did. For example you might think:

- I feel like dropping this candy wrapper on the ground instead of putting it in the garbage. What would happen if everyone did as I did? The street would be a mess.

- I think I should stop eating meat. What would happen if everyone did as I did? Well, there would be a lot of consequences for the earth's resources, the farming industry, and the rights of animals.

Universalizing like this can help you decide whether the act is ethical or not.

A. Universalize to decide whether the following acts are ethical:

    i)   I am thinking about hitting Leon because he was rude to Sophie.

    ii)   I am thinking about smoking a cigarette.

    iii)   I am thinking about converting to solar power.

    iv)   I am thinking about plagiarizing on my history assignment.

    v)   I am thinking about studying less.

    vi)   I am thinking about lying on my resume.

B. If you lived in a world where everyone did the following things, would you do them? Why/why not?

    i)   Shook hands with their left hands instead of their right

    ii)   "Borrowed" other people's property and often forgot to give it back

    iii)   Didn't eat meat

    iv)   Viciously attacked each other on Saturday evenings for fun

    v)   Traded girlfriends/boyfriends every week

    vi)   Cut off all communication with their parents at the age of 15 years

    vii)   Cheated on exams

THE TERRORIST ATTACK

You are doing some work experience at a local chemical factory when terrorists break in and hold everyone hostage. Then they single you out.

A. They tell you to open the company safe full of money or they will shoot you. Do you open the safe?

B. Three of them give you a gun and tell you to kill the factory manager or they will kill three hostages. If you try to shoot one of them, or yourself, they will shoot all the hostages. Do you shoot the factory manager?

C. They tell you to make a video saying "America is evil and deserves to be blown up" or they will shoot you. Do you do it?

D. They take you down to the storeroom in the factory. It turns out that chemicals are being stored there that can easily make weapons. If the terrorists get them they will use them to make bombs. They say that unless you give the chemicals to them they will shoot you and all of the hostages. Do you do it?

E. They load the chemicals into a getaway car. Then they force you to drive the car towards the local railway line. They plan to leave the car on the tracks. When a train crashes into it, it will blow up. They tell you if you do not drive the car, they will shoot you, and then drive the car themselves. Do you drive the car to the railway line?

EUTHANASIA

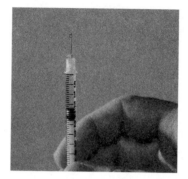

Euthanasia is the act of ending another person's life, usually in order to end their suffering. This may or may not be done with the person's consent. Imagine you are a judge for an "Ethical Medical Tribunal" and you have to decide whether to punish the following people for committing euthanasia.

A. Mr. Blanchard's wife was in severe and incurable pain. She suffered from a terrible illness that meant she was unable to move. Her life expectancy was six months. She could still speak, but barely. Over a one-month period, she repeatedly asked her husband to kill her. He purchased a drug that painlessly kills people and injected her with it. She died.

    i)   Should Mr. Blanchard be punished for his actions?

    ii)   Should he have done what he did?

iii) Would it make a difference on Mr. Blanchard's case if:

- his wife only had six days to live?

- his wife was not in pain, but was still sick and uncomfortable in the hospital?

- his wife had a life insurance policy worth five million dollars?

- his children did not want their mother to die, even if Mrs. Blanchard made it clear she did?

B. Mr. Taylor's wife was in severe and incurable pain with a debilitating illness and a six-month life expectancy. However, she was not able to not communicate. Mr. Taylor injected his wife with a drug that killed her.

i) Should Mr. Taylor be punished for his actions?

ii) Should he have done what he did?

C. What is your own view regarding euthanasia? Is it ethical? Do the following arguments help how you think about it?

- FOR: People have a *right* to die when they choose, particularly if they are in serious pain and they have little or no chance of ever being freed from it.

- AGAINST: God (of whatever belief) put us on the earth for a purpose and a lifespan. It is not up to us to choose the time of our own dying.

- FOR: Euthanasia does not harm anyone else except the person who chooses to have someone assist him to die.

- AGAINST: Euthanasia is a slippery slope—once we accept the concept of euthanasia, we may then accept it for people who are in *less* pain or people who are simply old, tired of life, or depressed.

- FOR: Without current medical technology many of the people with these conditions would have already died.

ETHICS IN BUSINESS—
ZEN BRACELETS

You are on the board of the surf clothing company "Wetware." You have done the almost impossible and made 1980s boardshorts and wetsuits the height of fashion again. Your firm is listed on the stock exchange and has several hundred shareholders. Each member of the board owns a few percent of the shares too. Your firm is seen as cutting edge and is a style icon amongst teenagers up and down the coast.

You have recently explored extending into iconic, ionic (but not ironic) "Mother-Zen" bracelets that claim to give you balance and help you to stay on your surfboard. Your proposed $20 ionic "Mother Zen" bracelet is merely a piece of plastic that costs $.20 to make in a factory. It comes with a holographic square.

Your marketing gurus have written the following ad for it: "Our extra cool bracelet exploits the holographic powers known for centuries amongst the Buddhist tribes of Sumatra. It also relies on the scientifically tested 'Placebo effect.' Look cool on the beach and keep your balance on the board with Mother Zen."

Adam Blair, the latest cage fighting star has agreed to endorse the bracelet, saying "It gives me balance even in the scariest cages."

A. Do you go ahead with selling and marketing these bracelets? Why/why not?

B. Do you use the above statements as marketing pitches for teenagers? Why/why not?

C. What are your duties to:

    i)   your shareholders to make money?

    ii)   your customers not to make misleading statements?

    iii)   society?

94

BUSINESS ETHICS — COMPETITION

You are on the board of the surf clothing company "Wetware." You have done the almost impossible and made 1980s boardshorts and wetsuits the height of fashion again. Your firm is listed on the stock exchange and has several hundred shareholders. Each member of the board owns a few percent of the shares too. Your firm is seen as cutting edge and is a style icon amongst teenagers up and down the coast. You set up a shop in your town.

A. "Granny Betty's Goode Olde Surf Shop" has existed in your town for 80 years. A lease comes up for the giant mega-shop next door to her shop. Opening up next door will very likely have the effect of shutting down her surf store. Do you take the lease? What are your duties to:

i)   your shareholders?

ii)   your customers?

iii) Granny Betty?

iv) the people who go to the beach?

v)   all of society?

B. In a stroke of good fortune five shops become available in your town. All five of them are next door to the five current surf shops in your town. Do you take up all five leases and then have a massive sale in each of your five shops to drive the other five shops out of business? Once the other five shops are gone you will be the only surf shop in your town. What are your duties to:

i)   your shareholders?

ii)   your customers?

iii) the people who own the other shops?

iv) the people who go to the beach?

v)   all of society?

ETHICAL THINKER— LAWRENCE KOHLBERG AND HEINZ'S DILEMMA

Note: the conversations ending in a 5 (i.e. 15, 25, 35) are a little different. They focus on what famous ethical philosophers in the past have thought. They will challenge your understanding of ethics and improve your thinking.

Lawrence Kohlberg was a moral philosopher who thought that people's ethical development progressed through six stages. He thought that the most ethical people got all the way to Stage Six, but that others got caught somewhere between what he called Stages One and Five.

He also made up a moral dilemma, which he called "Heinz's Dilemma." The various answers to this dilemma were supposed to link to each of the six stages of moral reasoning.

The dilemma is presented as a short and easy play below (read it to yourself or out loud).

LAME-O THEATRE" PRESENTS. . .
HEINZ'S DILEMMA!!!

CHARACTERS:
MR. HEINZ : MRS. HEINZ : PROFESSOR EVIL

The left hand side of the stage: Heinz's bedroom
The right hand side of the stage: Professor Evil's laboratory

SCENE 1: Heinz's bedroom
Heinz is sitting in a chair, reading a paper. His wife stands beside him.

Heinz: Hey, look at this article in the paper. It says that our beautiful country village has just gone for 100 years without a single crime being committed.

Mrs. Heinz: That's lovely darling, but I'm feeling faint.
Heinz ignores her and keeps reading the paper. He suddenly gasps in shock.

Heinz: Look here! It says here that the purple pustulant death is sweeping the country.

Mrs. Heinz: Oh dear, I feel ill.

Heinz: (ignoring her) It says that everyone who gets it dies.

Mrs. Heinz: Gosh. I can feel lumps coming up on my arms.

Heinz: And it says that Dr. Evil has perfected a cure but refuses to give it to anyone.

Mrs. Heinz: I'm going to be sick.
Mrs. Heinz collapses on the floor. Heinz looks down in shock.

Heinz: Good lord! My darling wife has the purple pustulant death!

SCENE 2: Professor Evil's Laboratory

Professor Evil is making some concoction at a bench. There is a bottle of clear liquid on the table. Heinz knocks on the door. Professor Evil lets him in.

Professor Evil: How can I help you? (maniacal laugh)

Heinz: My wife has contracted the purple pustulant death!

Professor Evil: How sad for you! (rubs hands and laughs maniacally)

Heinz: And you have invented a cure. Could I please have it?

Professor Evil: Certainly.
Professor Evil picks up the bottle of liquid on the table. He goes to hand it to Heinz.

Professor Evil: That will be one million dollars. (laughs maniacally)

Heinz: I can't afford that! Even if I sold all my house and property, I would only get a quarter of that.

Professor Evil: Too bad.

Heinz: But don't you care about my wife?

Professor Evil: Not at all. Not one jot. Not one iota.

Heinz: Professor Evil, you are evil!

Professor Evil: Look boyo, I didn't invent the cure because I cared about anyone. I invented the cure because I was interested in the science. Now the cure is mine. I can charge you 20 dollars, or a million dollars, or just tip it down the sink. Because it's MINE, all MINE! I can do whatever I want with the cure because without me, it wouldn't even exist in the first place.

Heinz: You monster! I am leaving.

SCENE 3: Heinz's bedroom

Heinz's wife lies on a bed, coughing, spluttering, and looking purple.

Heinz: My poor, poor dear. Professor Evil would not sell me the cure. He is so evil.

Heinz's wife tries to look brave, but just coughs.

Heinz: I will do something. I will steal the drug!

Heinz's wife: No darling. Do not do that. (coughs) Nobody has committed a crime in this town for 100 years. If you start, where will it stop? (coughs)

Heinz: I do not care for such things.

Heinz's wife: If you steal, you will be banished from the town and will have to wander the wasteland, friendless and alone.

Heinz: Oh, no. What a dilemma!

SCENE 4: Outside Professor Evil's Laboratory

Heinz creeps up to the door. Professor Evil has fallen asleep on the floor inside the laboratory.

Heinz looks tortured and confused.

A. Should Heinz steal the drug?

B. Look at the six stages of ethical development on the next page. Try to come up with a reason for or against Heinz stealing the drug based on of each of the levels of development.

STAGE ONE: Punishment
Obey the law so that you won't get punished. Right is what is not punished.

STAGE TWO: Get something
Obey the law to gain something for yourself (and so you won't get caught). Right is what satisfies your needs.

STAGE THREE: Approval
Obey the law so you can gain other people's approval. Right is what pleases the whole group.

STAGE FOUR: Law and order
Obey the law because the law says so and you should uphold the law. Right is showing respect for authority and maintaining the social order.

STAGE FIVE: Social contract
Obey the law because society has agreed that these laws are generally a good idea. Right is what has been thought hard about and agreed on by society.

STAGE SIX: Universal ethical principles
Obey the law because it respects human worth, individuality, and reciprocity. Right is what conforms you to abstract concepts of justice and ethics.

BUSINESS ETHICS — STAFF

You are on the board of the surf clothing company "Wetware." You have done the almost impossible and made 1980s boardshorts and wetsuits the height of fashion again. Your firm is listed on the stock exchange and has several hundred shareholders. Each member of the board owns a few percent of the shares too. Your firm is seen as cutting edge and is a style icon amongst teenagers up and down the coast.

A. You have your surfwear made by a factory in South America. You have made some attempts to do business with factories in China but it hasn't worked out. A California-based businessman with contacts in Guangdong Province in China says that he can get you the same quality materials for half the price. He has several (verified) references from long-established clothing firms saying that he delivers what he promises. You ask about conditions in the factories and whether they use child labor. He says that you can trust him to make proper enquiries. He also claims that it won't be your ethical responsibility, it will be his.

i) Do you take his offer to have your clothing made in a factory in Guangdong?

ii) Do you do something else?

iii) Who are you ethically responsible to?

iv) What are your ethical obligations?

B. You do not like one of the sales representatives in your shop. She does an okay job, neither great nor terrible, but the two of you just don't "click." You find her jokes boring, her dress sense appalling and frankly, you don't think she is very smart at all. However, she does a perfectly okay job. Her 12-month "probation" period comes up.

i) Do you re-employ her?

ii) What are your obligations?

C. You pay your sales staff $65,000 each year, including benefits such as holidays and health care. It turns out that if you fired them all and employed people as hourly (day-by-day employment) you could employ each person for $40,000 a year.

i) What should you do?

ii) What do you do?

CONVERSATION
97
SECRETS

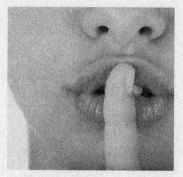

A. If you get in trouble at school for being bad in class, should you tell your parents? When? Why?

B. If your parents knew that a small meteor was going to fall out of the sky in six months and turn you into dust, should they tell you now? Should they tell you at all?

C. If people are being bad to you at school, should you tell your parents? Why?

D. Are there things your parents shouldn't know about you? If so, what?

E. Are there things that you shouldn't tell your parents? Are there things that your parents shouldn't tell you?

F. Are there things about you that your parents shouldn't tell you?

G. If everyone but your best friend has been invited to a party (and she doesn't know about it), should you tell her about it?

H. If one of your friends has stolen an iPod from someone else in the class and they have told you, would you keep it a secret?

I. You are friends with Julie. Maxine is also supposedly friends with Julie. However, Maxine tells other people at school that Julie smells and is ugly. Do you tell Julie what Maxine is saying?

J. Your best friend asks you if you can keep a secret. You say, "Yes." She then tells you that her mother hits her and she has bruises. Do you keep this secret?

K. When is it more important to "keep a secret" and when is it more important to "tell the truth?"

98

FIGHTING

A. Peter has vandalized your bag, poured water on your books, spat on your face, and told your friends you are weak. He challenges you to a fight.

i) He is a larger and stronger than you. Do you fight him? Why/why not?

ii) He is the same size and strength as you. Do you fight him? Why/why not?

iii) He is smaller and weaker than you. Do you fight him? Why/why not?

iv) What other things could/should you do about Peter?

B. Peta has vandalized your bag, poured water on your books, spat on your face, and told your friends you are weak. She challenges you to a fight. She is about the same size and strength as you. Do you fight her?

C. Why do some people fight? Why do people not fight?

D. Is fighting to protect someone else okay?

E. Is a fight okay if both people like fighting and agree to do it?

F. Why is assault illegal?

G. What would the following be like if most people thought that fighting was a good way to solve problems?

    i)   your school

    ii)   your suburb

    iii) the world

H. If people fight to solve issues when they are young, how do they solve problems when they are older? Is this good?

I. Imagine you are playing in a park. A bully comes over and hits you. Your father shouts at him and tells him off. The bully's father then runs over and shouts at your father to either fight him or get out of the park. What should your father do?

99

SHARING

A. Every day you take chips to school as part of lunch. Every day your best friend takes 10 or 12 chips from you. She never has anything in her lunch worth eating. Is it fair of her to keep taking the chips?

B. Your best friend gets $100 pocket money every week. You get $5. Should he treat for your food and drinks each time you go out together?

C. What if everyone did it?

    i) Describe what your school would be like if everyone shared all of their possessions (think of the good and the bad things).

ii) Describe what your school would be like if no one shared any of their possessions (think of the good and the bad things).

iii) Which of these two situations would you rather live in?

D. Should your parents share the following things with you?

i) their money

ii) their house

iii) their music collections

iv) use of a prized object (e.g. electric guitar)

v) the special, extra tasty food they have bought

vi) their alcoholic drinks or cigarettes

E. Whenever you start playing with something, your little sister asks to have a turn (even if she hasn't played with the thing for weeks). Should you share?

F. What has been the hardest thing you have ever had to share? Why was it hard?

G. What are three things you own that you would be happy to share? What are three things you own that you wouldn't want to share? What are the differences between these things?

H. Should you share friends with your younger brother/sister? If your older sister is going to a concert that you are dying to see with her best friend, should she take you too?

CONVERSATION
100

FRIENDSHIP
(PART TWO)

A. Should you have to go to a best friend's party, even if there is a much better party on at the same time?

B. If a friend of yours went overseas and you didn't stay in touch, would they still be your friend? Could you still go and stay at their house overseas after three or four years apart?

C. Imagine that a good friend of yours is very emotional and tells you "We're not friends anymore." However, he has told you that six times before already and each time you have made up. Are the two of you still friends, even if he says you are not?

D. When a friendship ends, is someone usually to blame? Can the end of a friendship ever be a good thing?

E. If there is a shy person in your class without any friends, is it your responsibility to help them? Or is making friends up to them?

F. If there is a person in your class, who can't speak any English, without any friends, is it your responsibility to help them? Is it your responsibility to become a friend of theirs?

(See also Conversation 46: Friendship (part one))

101

HOW TO SPREAD STUFF AROUND (PART ONE)

You and your family are sent to live on the island of Microcosm. You don't yet know what jobs your parents are going to have. It turns out there are only ten jobs on the whole island; everything else is done by machine. The leader of Microcosm tells you that, according to the law, the newest people on the island get to decide what salary everyone earns for the next year. You don't know what they earned in previous years. You have one million dollars to split among all of the workers.

A. How do you split the money up among the following ten jobs, all of which take up 40 hours per week?

i) farmer
ii) garbage collector
iii) doctor
iv) nurse
v) lawyer
vi) leader
vii) banker
viii) novelist
ix) teacher
x) builder

B. Do some jobs deserve more money than others? If so, why? How do you decide which ones deserve more or less?

CONVERSATION

102

HOW TO SPREAD STUFF AROUND (PART TWO)

A. Your teacher brings 200 Easter eggs to school and puts them in the middle of the classroom. "Take whatever you want" she says and leaves the room. There is a mad scramble for the Easter eggs. Some people end up with dozens, others only with two or three. When she comes back, people in the class complain that the eggs were distributed unfairly.

"How should I have done it?" she asks.

"Each person should have been given an equal amount" you say.

"Okay," she replies. "I'll remember that for next time."

Half an hour later your teacher exclaims "Oh no, I need 60 of those Easter eggs to give to the choir after school." Then she says, "Okay, let's do this fairly. Everybody should have to return an equal amount. This means everyone gives two eggs back."

Is what your teacher has done fair? Why/why not?

B. Chris and Alex work equally hard as house painters. They are the same age and are equally experienced. However, Chris is twice as good at it as Alex. Chris finishes two houses in the time it takes Alex to finish one house.

  i) Should Chris get paid twice as much?

  ii) Should Chris only work half the number of hours in a day?

  iii) Should they get the same amount as they are both working hard?

C. If you were the boss of a company and you could choose how your workers got paid, how would you do it?

  i) Depending on how good they are or how much ability they have

  ii) Depending on how long they have been with the company

  iii) Depending on how hard they work

  iv) Depending on how much they need the money

PETS (PART ONE)

A. Briony has been asking for a pet dog for Christmas. She promises to take it for a walk every day. Her parents give in and buy her a puppy which she calls "Scamper." Within six months she is bored with Scamper and refuses to take him for a walk. What should Briony's parents do? If Briony absolutely refuses to walk Scamper no matter what happens, should her parents take Scamper for walks each day? If no one else wants the dog, could they take Scamper to the dog pound?

B. Would there be anything wrong with having the following animals as pets if your yard was big enough? What is the difference between them?

   i)   cat

   ii) caterpillar

   iii) elephant

   iv) python

   v)   dolphin

C. Are there any animals that it would be unfair to keep as pets? Which ones are they and why would it be unfair?

PETS (PART TWO)

A. Is it okay to keep a huge dog in a small yard if you feed it, walk it, and pet it every day? Why/why not?

B. Is it okay to buy a cat if you live on a main road and there is a good chance that the cat will wander out and get run over? Why/why not?

C. If you got some pet mice, is it okay to completely ignore them as long as they get enough food? Why/why not?

D. Some people think that we should not use animals for any reason, such as food or clothes, and this includes having animals as pets. They say that animals should only live in the wild and that it destroys an animal's dignity to be "owned" by a person. What do you think of this point of view? Why?

MARTIN LUTHER KING, JR. AND NON-VIOLENCE

Martin Luther King, Jr. is well known as an activist and civil rights leader. Underlying his actions was a philosophy of nonviolence. This was inspired by Mahatma Ghandi in India. He wrote about non-violence in his book *Stride Toward Freedom*.

Non-violence means that you should protest against injustice (particularly in his case, racism) peacefully. This is even if other people are being violent towards you. So, no matter how much your people are beaten, assaulted, and killed, you do not 'hit back' with violence of your own.

This happened to King and his followers. When they protested about racism in some of the Southern states, they were regularly beaten, attacked, firebombed, and even murdered.

The six principles of nonviolence according to King are:

1. Nonviolence is a way of life for courageous people. King thought that non-violence used all of the best features of a person's character.

2. The Beloved Community is the framework for the future. This was the 'final aim' of King—a society where everyone can achieve their full potential without poverty, no matter what race they are.

3. Attack forces of evil, not persons doing evil. This meant that you couldn't be violent to the actual people who were oppressing or attacking you.

4. Accept suffering without retaliation for the sake of the cause to achieve the goal. Accepting suffering, King thought, gave you moral authority. It also helps your cause grow.

5. Avoid internal violence of the spirit as well as external physical violence. This meant that the people practising non-violence should not feel bitter or angry about their attackers either.

6. The universe is on the side of justice. This means 'the moral arc of the universe is long but it bends towards justice.' If you practice nonviolence you are part of the right order of the Universe—and in the long term, more likely to overcome.

This section about King is based on material from The King Center's website: http://www.thekingcenter.org/king-philosophy

QUESTIONS

A. King states (No. 3) you should not be violent towards the people doing the violence towards you in demonstrations.

i) Is this possible?

ii) Are the people doing violence victims too?

iii) Can you think of a cause important enough to you that you would be willing to be beaten up and/or killed for it?

B. King says (No. 4) you should accept suffering to achieve the goal. Do you think that accepting suffering would make your cause more likely to succeed? Why/how?

C. King says (No. 6) that the universe is just. Do you believe that the universe bends towards justice? Or is it blind?

D. A fierce critic of King would say that the philosophy of non-violence isn't smart. If you are a non-violent organiser in a violent state you know that there is going to be violence and murder—it's just going to be against your own friends and people who trust you. Organizing for your friends to go out to be beaten and killed is worse than killing or hurting those who are oppressing you. What do you think?

E. If a bully hits you in the playground, should you hit them back?

F. If a government oppresses your people and shoots you when you have demonstrations, should you:

i) accept that they are a bad government and just try to get on with your life?

ii) continue to protest peacefully with other people in the hope of bringing the government down?

iii) protest with weapons, so that you can attack the police and army?

iv) plan to blow up government buildings and/or assassinate government leaders?

v) something else?

Why?

106

RIGHTS AND RESPONSIBILITIES

A. Many people say that rights and responsibilities are connected: that you need one in order to have the other. For example, your right not to be beat up at school hinges on your responsibility not to beat up anyone else at school.

  i)   If you beat up someone at school, do you lose your right not to be beat up?

  ii) If you don't hurt anyone at school, do you have *more* rights not be hurt at school?

  iii) If you behave very well in class, does the school have a responsibility to put you in a class where everyone behaves?

iv) If you behave badly in class, do you lose your right to be with people who behave well in class?

B. Can you have a right without any responsibility?

C. Jane called the town mayor, "A liar, a cheat, and a crook." She had no evidence for this accusation. When challenged about this, she said "I have a right to freedom of speech." Does she have this right? Is she right to use freedom of speech in this way?

D. Ferdinand pays no attention at all to politics. He doesn't even know the name of the president. When he went to vote at the election, he voted for a party with blue pamphlets because blue was his favorite color. Does he have a right to vote?

E. For years Maria gave money to everyone else in the street when they couldn't afford food or clothes. Then Maria's company went broke and she was penniless. Does she have a right to expect other people in the street to give her food and clothes?

F. Josef wants to start a political party called the "shut down democracy" party. He proposes stopping freedom of speech and imprisoning all people who disagree with him. When people protest about this, he says "It is my democratic right in America to start any political party I want." Does he have a right to start this party? Does he have a responsibility to start up a party that respects democracy? Does the American government have a right to shut down this party?

VIOLENT COMPUTER  GAMES

A. What do many children know that their parents don't about the cyber world? What could parents know that their children may not know? How can parents and children have a good discussion about online things when their levels of knowledge are very different?

B. Some violent video games have an "MA" or "R" rating. Should people be able to play these games before they are 18 years of age? Why/why not? Why are these restrictions in place?

C. What do you think happens when people play violent video games? Do they become more violent themselves? Is it ethical to produce, sell, or play extremely violent video games?

D. Should people be able to see "MA" or "R" rated movies before they are 18 years of age? Why are these restrictions in place? Should the parents be able to decide? Why/why not?

DESIGNER BABIES
(PART ONE)

You have been transported to the future. Because the government thinks you are "ethically pure" you have been put in charge of their "Medical Ethics Tribunal." But things are a bit different in the future. Babies can be genetically "designed" like recipe books. The following people come to your ethics tribunal and you have to decide whether to let them design their babies.

What do you decide in each case?

A. Mr. and Mrs. Richards both have hemophilia, which is genetically passed on. There is a 100% chance that their child will have hemophilia. They ask you to allow them to alter the gene so that their child is not a hemophiliac.

B. Mr. and Mrs. Felton have a cluster of genes in their family that will make it more likely that their child will become diabetic later in life. They ask you to allow them to alter their genes so that their child cannot become a diabetic later in life.

C. Mr. and Mrs. Jones lost their child at the age of five. Using samples from their child they have had made a genetically exact zygote (single cell). They wish to implant this zygote into Mrs. Jones to have a genetically identical child. They ask you for permission to do this.

D. Mr. and Mrs. Hunchback of Notre Dame have come to you with a zygote from another couple. This other couple have three other intelligent and beautiful children. Mr. and Mrs. Hunchback tell you that they do not want their child to be cursed with their own deformities and they would like him/her to be blessed with natural advantages. They ask you permission for this other zygote to be implanted in Mrs. Hunchback.

DESIGNER BABIES
(PART TWO)

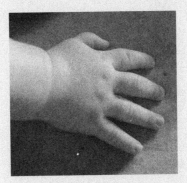

You have been transported to the future. Because the government thinks you are "ethically pure" you have been put in charge of their "Medical Ethics Tribunal." But things are a bit different in the future. Babies can be genetically "designed" like recipe books. You are now on your second day at work. The following people come to your ethics tribunal and you have to decide whether to let them design their babies.

What do you decide in each case?

A. Mrs. and Mrs. Mansfield both have grotesquely large noses and they are aware that their child will probably have an even more grotesquely large nose. They ask for permission to alter their genes so that their child will have a nose that is smaller than theirs.

B. Mr. and Mrs. Mackay would like their child to have a straight and well-proportioned nose. They ask for permission to alter their genes to allow this to happen.

C. Mr. and Mrs. Smith come to you. They bring a genetic formula with them that would allow their child to be:

- intelligent

- attractive

- very good at sports

- a very good piano player

They ask you to insert this formula into a zygote (single cell) and so design their baby.

D. In general when, if ever, do you think that that the genes of a zygote should be changed?

E. What would a society look like in which everyone designed their babies? Would it be a wonderful place full of almost perfect people, or would it be something else?

CONVERSATION 40: ETHICAL POTHOLES AT DUDGEON HIGH

Conversation 1: Everyone does it

Conversation 2: They're too big to notice

Conversation 3: If you can't beat them, join them

Conversation 4: It's not my fault

Conversation 5: It's not the worst thing

Conversation 6: It's not illegal

Conversation 7: The letter of the law

Conversation 8: Poor me, I'm under a lot of stress

Conversation 9: It's what my heart tells me

Conversation 10: If I don't do it someone else will

Conversation 11: They deserved it

Conversation 12: Eye for an eye

Conversation 13: It's too small to count

Conversation 14: Cognitive dissonance

Conversation 15: I'm good

Conversation 16: The ends justify the means